Broken Promises, Broken Dreams:
Disparities and Disappointments.
Civil Rights in the 21st Century

Stephen Balkaran

Copyright 2017
Published by: Kiwi Publishing, Inc.
Post Office Box 3852
Woodbridge, CT 06525
info@kiwipublishing.com
www.kiwipublishing.com
203-295-0370

No part of this book may be reproduced or transmitted in any form, by any means, electronic or mechanical, including photocopying, recording, or by an information storage and retrieval system, without written permission from the publisher.

Limit of Liability/Disclaimer of Warranty: While the publisher and authors have used their best efforts in preparing this book, they make no representations or warranties with respect to the accuracy or completeness of the contents of this book and specifically disclaim any implied warranties of merchantability or fitness for a particular purpose.

No warranty may be created or extended by sales representatives or writ- ten sales materials. The advice and strategies contained herein may not be suitable for your situation. You should consult a professional when appropriate. Neither the publisher nor the author shall be liable for any loss of profit or any other commercial damages, including but not limited to special, incidental, consequential, or other damages.

ISBN 13 978-1-935768-21-0
First Edition: 2017
Printed in the United States on recycled paper
Cover design and book layout by Kiwi Publishing

"Civil Rights remain the pinnacle of debates, protecting rights regardless of color, race, ethnicity, religion, or sexual orientation, and defending these rights against discrimination have long been an important issue in America. Some fifty years later after the passage of the Civil Rights Act of 1964, has our government has defaulted on that promise? African-Americans and other minority groups remain one of the most underrepresented communities in schools, workforce, and other sectors in the American society."

Stephen Balkaran.

<u>The Continuing Significance of Race: An American Dilemma.</u>

Permission

The following institutions and places are kindly acknowledge for their permission for following the use of the portraits, monuments, photos, and other Civil Rights Memorabilia.

The City of Birmingham. AL
The King Center for Non Violence & Peace. Atlanta, GA
The Carter Center. Atlanta, GA
The National Civil Rights Museum. Memphis. TN

For all those that are not mentioned, I kindly acknowledge the gratitude for allowing the use of any Civil Rights Memorabilia.

Thank you.

Stephen Balkaran

Acknowledgements

Dedicated to all those who have fought for the guaranteed rights under the Constitution of the United States during the Institution of Slavery, Jim Crow, Civil Rights era in the 1960's and the 21st Century. My family, friends here in the United States, Trinidad & Tobago, and those that have supported my ideas of non-violence, the philosophy of Mahatma Gandhi, and Dr. Martin L. King.

Special acknowledgments to Michael B. Taylor for his continued support and advice. Last and no means least, all the Academic Institutions in Connecticut that have played an important role in shaping my entire academic life.

Dedicated to Victoria N. Ward.
2016 Babe Ruth World Series Participant

Dedicated to Jason T. Bajorek and
Dr. Winston E. Thompson

RIP, Gone but never forgotten.

"To everything there is a season, and a time to every purpose under the heaven: a time to be born and a time to die: a time to weep, and a time to mourn, and a time to dance."

-Ecclesiastes III

Table of Contents

Preface — 1

Chapter 1 — 5
Race

Chapter 2 — 19
Poverty

Chapter 3 — 39
Black Lives Matter

Chapter 4 — 47
Education

Chapter 5 — 75
Immigration

Chapter 6 — 79
Criminal Justice System

Chapter 7 — 105
Healthcare Disparities

Chapter 8 — 131
Hate Crimes

Chapter 9 — 145
The Politics of Race, Immigration Reform, and the 2016 Presidential Election

Chapter 10 — 163
Conversations on Race, Truth, and Reconciliation in America

Chapter 11 — 171
Conclusion

About the Author — 177

Preface

> *"Any nation that spends more money on military defense and weapons than on social uplift programs is approaching a spiritual doom."*
> Martin Luther King. Jr.[1]

Civil Rights continues to be the pinnacle of debates under our first African-American President, protecting rights regardless of color, race, ethnicity, religion, or sexual orientation, and defending these rights against discrimination have long been an important issue in America. Some fifty years later, after the passage of the Civil Rights Act of 1964, has our government defaulted on that promise? African-Americans and other minority groups remain one of the most underrepresented communities in schools, workforce, and other sectors in the American society.

During the summer of 2010, while in Atlanta, GA on my Civil Rights Project, I had the opportunity to interview Martin Luther King III on his father's legacy and Civil Rights. This interview led to the much anticipated question on how would his dad, the late Civil Rights leader, Dr. Martin Luther King Jr, react on the progress of African-Americans in the 21st Century? His candid, but critical response was *"Dismayed and Disappointed"* African-Americans; he claimed lag far behind all ethnic groups in every possible avenues of the American life. Hence, the ideas started on the critical analysis of the famed Civil Rights Movement and assessing the outcomes on the greatest social movement in modern history. Some fifty years later, after the passage of the Civil Rights Act of 1964, which is arguably one of the most important legislative acts in our country's history. Has our government defaulted on that promise? Is the American dream still in reach in many black and brown communities, or has a history of exclusion, racism, and oppression replaced that dream?

The Civil Rights Movement which started for social equality and later became an economic priority with the Dr. King's Poor Peoples Campaign has truly been a disappointment for both social and economic integration of African-Americans into the American society. Some fifty years after the historic Civil Rights Movement and Civil Rights Act of 1964, racial disparities in income, education, health care, incarceration, racial profiling, hate crimes, and home ownership have increased and by many outlooks are continuing to grow at alarming rates between the races. The history of America has been closely pegged with racism and discrimination against African-Americans, it's an issue the founding fathers struggled to address in the early stage of the great nation. As a result, it has continued to haunt our society during slavery, Jim Crow's segregation, and modern day legalized and systematic racism. This history is a 300-year struggle against racism and oppression in a country that still today refuses to acknowledge and apologize for its wrongdoing. African-Americans have contributed in every avenue of American life, since the inception of this great country economically, socially, and politically; they have carved their contribution into the American society. Militarily, African-Americans continue to play a vital role in every conflict, in every war, in every battle, and on every battlefield. African-Americans have put their lives on the line to protect freedom, liberty, and democracy in the Revolutionary War, Civil War, World War I and II, Vietnam, and the present day war in Iraq-Afghanistan. African-Americans have always met the challenge of serving America with great pride, commitment, and admiration. Yet, despite this remarkable contribution, African-Americans are continually treated as second-class citizens. This treatment has perpetuated a deep uncertainty as to who African-Americans really are and has led to many African-Americans being excluded from the American dream.

Despite this commitment to America, their acceptance into society remains a distant second with historical racism and segregation that dates back to the 1620's, when the first slave plantation in what was then the colony of Virginia, began experimenting with black slaves. In the 21st century we continue to see many facets of oppression that exist and are prevalent in American society. Since the inception of America, the house of democracy has been plagued with cracks of racism and discrimination against African-Americans and women. During the last 300 years America has made little attempts to fix these cracks and, as a result, America has struggled with a flawed foundation. Thus, here lies the problem of why race and Civil Rights still matters in America. America has strayed away from The Civil Rights Movement's legacy of advancing the opportunities for African-Americans, guaranteeing their constitutional rights, eradicating legalized, systematic racism throughout the nation, and more so, the leveling of the playing-field for everyone.

The election of our first African-American President in 2008 showed the progress we have made towards racial reconciliation. The fact that 55% of white Americans voted for an African-American candidate showed the healing of a nation, but more so showed the positive progress towards racial tolerance. Despite this historic movement towards racial reconciliation, integration of the races has left a blind eye to many of the social disparities that Dr. King and the Civil Rights Movement, vowed to dismantle. Legalized and systematic racism has replaced overt racism as the major cancer of American society. In fact, Black Lives Matter is an example of the new Civil Rights Movement that has taken up the mantle of the famed 1960's movement.

Vice President Hubert Humphrey once remarked that the passage of the Civil Rights Act of 1964 was America's greatest FOREIGN POLICY, letting the rest of the world know that our commitment to peace, equality, justice for African-Americans, and other minority communities would be the cornerstone of American democracy. Some fifty years later, WHERE ARE WE with regard to America's greatest Foreign Policy?

Chapter 1
Race

"I wish I could say that racism and prejudice were only distant memories. We must dissent from the indifference. We must dissent from the apathy. We must dissent from the fear, the hatred and the mistrust... We must dissent because America can do better, because America has no choice but to do better."
-Thurgood Marshall. 1992[1]

Race discussions and America's post racial society has left a silence gap in one of most debatable topics to emerge in the twenty-first century; that is, post racial America in the age of President Barack Obama. No other time in our country's great history has an idea of a post racial society caught the eye of many Americans. Many argue the emergence of an African-American candidate has fuel the debate regarding where do the politics of race fit in America. As Barack Obama continues his presidency but lacks any commitment to discuss race indicates that America is not ready to have a constructive dialogue on race despite the election its first African-American President. Why hasn't America gone beyond the issue of Race and Civil Rights? The history of America has been closely pegged with racism and discrimination against African-Americans, it's an issue the founding fathers struggled to address in the early stage of this great nation and as a result it has continued to haunt our society during slavery, Jim Crow's segregation, Civil Rights movement and modern day legalized and systematic racism.

As we all looked on January 2009 when much of the world watched the swearing in of the first African-American president into office, the idea that America was willing to put its ugly past behind and move towards a post racial society and become a more tolerable nation where Dr. Martin L. King's dream would be fulfilled, enlightened all of us. Our increased expectations that America would transcend race and that both white and black racial attitude would undergo a fundamental change, but, it has not. The presence of the first African-American President and the first family has NOT alleviated racial stereotypes nor have they engaged in any constructive dialogue on race in America. The idea of a post racial America continues to be lost in transition; race and racism continue to be significant factors as we delve into the deep waters of race in America. As we enter the second phase of the Obama presidency, several important debates continue to haunt our society that has taken away the best of who we are as Americans. First and foremost, race and politics are alive and well in America, and second, post racial America continues to be a major disappointment as we have yet to leave our racist attitudes and mindset behind us.

Because of the visible and widespread contributions of African-American Civil Rights leaders, educators, architects, inventors, scientists, sports heroes, and others, many have wrongly assumed that these disparities have already been dismantled. The disparities in educational systems, poverty rates, in the criminal justice and other sectors of society continue to plague a country that promises so much yet guarantees so little. Why has race continued to play such a large role in America even fifty years after the enactment of the Civil Right Act in 1964? Since America's inception, its brand of democracy has been plagued with racial and gender discrimination. We have made few attempts to amend these democratic shortcomings during the last three hundred years, and as a result, we have struggled with a defective foundation. Therein lays the answer for why race still matters in America. Many Americans refuse to come to terms that the history of African-Americans is a struggle against racism and oppression in a country that even today continues to refuse to neither acknowledge nor apologize for its past wrongdoing. Our increased expectation that America would transcend race and that both white and black racial attitudes would undergo a fundamental change has not come to fruition. Some fifty years after the monumental Civil Rights Act of 1964, America continues to grapple with the issue of race and it continues to divide us as a nation.

Gone are the days of former Alabama Governor George C. Wallace, who famously preached, *"Segregation now! Segregation tomorrow! Segregation forever!"* to resounding applause in 1963.[2] Gone are the days when signs reading *"whites only"* and *"colored"* hung prominently over water fountains, bathrooms, and restaurant counters. However, in the twenty-first century, silent and not overt racism exists in our school systems, places of employment, healthcare systems, prison systems, immigrant communities, and other sectors of societies. It also permeates our society in ways we don't even realize and takes away the best of who we are and what we can become as a nation.

Race relations have always been an important issue in the struggle for equality and reconciliation in America. A recent Gallup poll from July 17, 2013, looked at Racial and Ethnic Relations in the United States found that, when white Americans were asked, *"Do you think that race relations between whites and blacks will always be a problem?"* forty percent of Americans said that race and black-white relations will always be a problem in the United States. Comparatively, in another survey conducted by Gallup poll in 1964, when the same question was posed to white Americans, forty-two percent believed that race and black-white relations will always be a problem in the United States.[3] Despite the election of our first African-American President, the research shows that little, if any, progress has occurred in the last fifty years when it comes to optimism towards race relations.

According to the Pew Research Center, almost eight years after Barack Obama's election as the nation's first black President–an event that engendered a sense of optimism among many Americans about the future of race relations, a series of flashpoints around the U.S. has exposed deep racial divides and reignited a national conversation about race. A new Pew Research Center survey finds profound differences between black and white adults in their views on racial discrimination, barriers to black progress and the prospects for change.[3] The report also concluded that overwhelming majority of blacks (88%) say the country needs to continue to making changes for blacks to have equal rights with whites, but 43% are skeptical that such changes will occur. More broadly, the Pew Center concluded that "blacks and whites offer different perspectives of the current state of race relations in the U.S. White Americans are evenly divided, with 46% saying race relations are generally good and 45% saying they are generally bad. In contrast, by a nearly two-to-one margin, blacks are more likely to say race relations are bad (61%) rather than good (34%). Blacks ae also about twice as likely to say too little attentions is paid to race and racial issues in the US." (58% vs. 27%)

As we celebrate the sixtieth anniversary of Justice Thurgood Marshall and the Supreme Court's decision in "<u>Brown v. Board of Education</u>"[4] on school desegregation. In the Brown decision in 1954, the notion of separate but equal was finally struck down. The former notion of separate but equal was built on the foundations of white supremacy, which provided legal justification for separation of the races, and required separate accommodations for whites and blacks in many U.S. states and cities, up until the 1960s. Despite the legalized eradication of school segregation, Harvard University's Civil Rights Project reported that schools today are more segregated than they were in the past. The report shows that U.S.

schools are becoming more segregated in all regions for both African-American and Latino students. The Civil Rights Project also reported that while we continue celebrating a legal victory over segregation, schools across the nation are becoming increasingly segregated.[5]

The Africana Studies and Research Center at Cornell University reported that in 1960, only twenty percent of the black population finished high school, compared with forty-three percent of the white population. Furthermore, only three percent of African-Americans graduated from college, less than half the white graduation rate of eight percent.[6] Some sixty years later, a 2013 report by the Journal of Blacks in Higher Education indicated that fifty-four percent of young African-Americans were graduating from high school, and forty-two percent of African-American students were graduating from college, still less than half the rate of white graduates. The report indicates that the vast majority of our nation's highest-ranked colleges and universities have shown significant improvement over the past quarter-century, but at the same time, there is a twenty percent gap in the graduation rate between white and black students.[7] Schools are becoming more segregated at a time when we hail public policies like, No Child Left Behind, Race to the Top and Common Core which promised quality and access to education for all, when in reality many black and brown kids are Left Behind.

The debates around education in America have become one of the forefront Civil Rights issue of the twenty-first century, disparities among white suburban, inner city black and brown students continue to be torn in society and has continue to define education in America. Some fifty years after President Lyndon B. Johnson declared *"War on Poverty,"* making poverty in America one of his top priorities during his presidency.[8] This not only raised awareness of poverty throughout American communities, but also ensured that early education, food stamps, and other government economic assistance programs would be extended to America's poor. Yet despite his great intention to raise this issue of poverty, and some fifty years after Dr. Martin L. King initiated his poor people's campaign in 1967, poverty continues to be the cancer that threatens our society and remains a significant inhibiting factor in many African-American households. According to the 2013 U.S. Census Bureau's report on Poverty in America, the poverty rate for African-Americans in 2013 was twenty-seven percent, which is an increase from twenty-five percent in 2005.[9] The report indicated that the poverty rate increased between 2005 and 2013 for every socioeconomic group within African-American families.

According to a study by the Pew Research Center, the wealth gaps between Caucasians and African-Americans are at an all-time high. The wealth of white households is 13 times the median of black households in 2013. This is the highest gap since 1989, when white households had seventeen times the wealth of African-Americans households.[10] There are a number of factors that contribute too many of the economic disparities that exist between African-American and Caucasian households including: access to economic opportunities, educational opportunities, systematic discrimination in employment, etc., which are still prevalent in society. Economic empowerment of the races has always been a cornerstone of American democracy, African-Americans economically continue to lag far behind other races, and a significant section of their community continues to struggle beyond the poverty threshold.

Recent events in Ferguson, MO, Baltimore, New York City and other race related incidents throughout the country have left many questions that continue to haunt our society.[11] The lost community policing, trust in law enforcement, treatment of young black males but more so the continuing significance of race in America. The recent riots that surrounded the death of both Michael Brown and Eric Garner have continued to open the debates about the discussions on race, criminal justice and America's commitment to a post racial society. These riots have brought many lingering racial issues to the surface, which can be only resolved by having more open dialogue on race and discussion of diversity in America. A recent poll by the New York Times revealed the race relation under the Obama Presidency is at an all-time low, *"Sixty-nine percent of Americans say race relations are generally bad, one of the highest levels of discord since the 1992 riots in Los Angeles during the Rodney King case, according to the latest New York Times/ CBS News poll."* [12] Despite any constructive dialogue by the President on race, relations between whites and blacks seem to have widen according the latest poll and the recent protest against police brutality.

The President remarks *"we not as divided as we seem, shows the stark difference in race attitudes in America, "the poll found that black and white Americans hold starkly different views on race, particularly regarding the treatment of African-Americans by the police. Asked whether the police in most communities are more likely to use deadly force against a black person than a white person, three-quarters of African-Americans answered yes, and only about half as many white people agree. Fifty-six percent of whites said that the race of the suspect made no difference in the use of force; only 18 percent of black Americans said so."* [13] With the election of our first African-American president, America has made great strides towards a more racially harmonious society, where all contributions to our great country despite the color of their skin are respected. Despite this optimism, race continues to play a defining role in who we are as Americans in the twenty-first century just as it did in the past. The failure to talk about race, racism, and the failure to acknowledge that racism exists in the twenty-first century, is what best defines one of the most contentious subjects in America. Thus we can now see in the twenty-first century there are still many facets of oppression that exist and are prevalent in American society and African-Americans continue to acknowledge that races continue to define us. As the nation's first African-American President concludes his tenure as leader of the free world, he has been met with a wide variety of critiques and praises. Center to the critiques are none more than the continued presence of Race in America, an issue that has left us more racially vulnerable than ever under his presidency. Many argue the election of America's first African-American President will fuel the debate around much needed racial tolerance, discord, and reconciliation that has engulfed our nation. As long as we are reminded about the President's words on racial reconciliation, *"One of the things that I've consistently said as president is that I'm the president of all people. I am very proud that my presidency can help to galvanize and mobilize America on behalf of issues of racial disparity and racial injustice,"* we are reminded that we must be vigilant and the fact that we still live in a society that still continues to exacerbate racial bigotry and hatred.

The election of the nation's first African-American President led to the increased expectations that America will put our ugly racial past behind and move forward into a more racially sensitive and tolerant society, which has enlightened all of us. The promise that America would transcend race and that both white and black racial attitude would undergo a fundamental positive and formative change, has NOT been fulfilled. The words of our President-elect in 2008, *"Change has come to America,"* has not materialized nor has it come to fruition. The nation's first African-American President has not elevated any racial tensions and misconceptions, but has perpetuated the continued racial divide that continue to define us and who we are. The dream that America would transcend race, and that racial attitude would undergo a fundamental change, has NOT materialized. The nation's first African-American President and his family have NOT alleviated racial stereotypes nor have they engaged in any constructive dialogue on race in America. The fact, that we all had great expectations and optimism that our President would ease the racial hatred after the 1950's and 1960's and promote a more racially tolerant society has NOT proven successful. Despite this increased expectation, under Obama's administration there has been more racial protest by African-Americans and others for justice and equality than the Civil Rights movement in the 1960's. Continued racial events in Ferguson, Missouri; New York City, New York; Baltimore, Maryland; Orlando, Florida; Charleston, South Carolina; and other parts of the country only reinforce America's immense racial hatred and the continued distrust in many African-American communities.

The persistent continuing of race riots throughout the country has left many questions that continue to haunt our society: Civil Rights, bigotry, hatred, but none more so important; the continuing significance of race in America. Racial hatred under Obama's administration has permeated our society in ways we don't even realize. It has continued to define who we are and what we stand for as nation that leads the free world and preaches democracy, rights and respect. The series of seemingly constant, mostly non-violent Black Lives Matter protests under President Obama's tenure has raised uncertainty on the rage, race, and rebellion that continue to plague many African-American communities. Race riots throughout Obama's administration have left many questions that continue to haunt our society: none more important than the continuing significance of race. The riots that surrounded the deaths of Michael Brown and others continue to open the debates about the discussions on race, profiling, bigotry, hatred, criminal justice, and America's post racial society. Unfortunately, this debate has neither materialized nor even blossomed, and any discussion on race takes away the best of who we are as Americans.

Thus, this continued dilemma, what we call race, can only be solved by the following steps despite who is or becomes the next leader of the free world: The need for America to have a more constructive dialogue on race has neither the past nor the future come to fruition for several factors. Any discussion of race among Americans elicits a very cautious and complicated reaction; many whites shy away from any racial dialogue. Second, the fact we need to admit we have a problem; a nation that is in denial and sleepwalking will never wake up. Third, Americans have refused to acknowledge that racism is a societal problem which can only be resolved by having more open dialogue on race, and discussions on diversity in America. Having an African-American President showed our ability to move beyond race and achieve racial reconciliation, but that will not solve, heel our racial past, nor resolve America's greatest social cancer; RACE.

Some fifty years after one of the greatest social movements in American history, African-Americans and other minority groups are still some of the most underrepresented groups in education, employment, criminal justice, and other sectors in American society. Post racial America has not come to fruition and the continuous disparities among the races, racial attitudes, stereotypes, racial profiling, and other elements in society have in many ways reinforced the significance of Race in the twenty-first century. In spite of the unquestioned greatness of America, there must be a conscious effort by all Americans to achieve some sought of racial reconciliation; we must acknowledge our past wrongdoings, and engage in conversations that can lead to a more racially tolerant society where America can be enjoyed by all.

References

1. Justice Thurgood Marshall. July 4TH, Speech 1992. Philadelphia. PA
   http://constitutioncenter.org/libertymedal/recipient_1992_speech.html
2. Governor George C. Wallace inaugural Speech. Montgomery, AL 1963
   http://web.utk.edu/~mfitzge1/docs/374/wallace_seg63.pdf
3. Gallup Poll Race Relations, July 17th 2013
   http://www.gallup.com/poll/163535/americans-rate-racial-ethnic-relations-positively.aspx
4. Brown v. Board of Education of Topeka, Kansas 347 U.S. 483 (1954)
   http://mlkpp01.stanford.edu/index.php/encyclopedia/encyclopedia/enc_brown_v_board_of_education_of_topeka_kansas_347_us_483_1954_349_us_294_/
5. Harvard University's Civil Rights Project: School Segregation on the Rise despite Growing Diversity among School-Aged Children."
   http://civilrightsproject.ucla.edu/research/k-12-education/integration-and-diversity/brown-at-50-king2019s-dream-or-plessy2019s-nightmare/?searchterm
6. Africana Studies and Research Center at Cornell University.
   http://www.asrc.cornell.edu/news/
7. The Journal of Blacks in Higher Education 2013 Report on Graduation rates
   http://www.jbhe.com/features/50_blackstudent_gradrates.html
8. President Lyndon B. Johnson, January 8, 1964. War on Poverty Speech.
   http://www.presidency.ucsb.edu/ws/?pid=26787
9. 2013 Census Report on Income and Poverty in the United States
   http://www.census.gov/prod/2013pubs/acsbr11-17.pdf

10. The Pew Research Center report on Wealth and Inequality. 2013 http://www.pewresearch.org/fact-tank/2014/12/12/racial-wealth-gaps-great-recession/
11. Michael Brown's event and CNN http://www.cnn.com/interactive/2014/08/us/ferguson-brown-timeline/
12. http://www.nytimes.com/2016/07/14/us/most-americans-hold-grim-view-of-race-relations-poll-finds.html?_r=1
13. Ibid

Bibliography:

1. Gallup Poll. Race Relations, July 17th 2013. July, 2013.
2. Harvard University's Civil Rights Project: School Segregation on the Rise despite Growing Diversity among School-Aged Children." 2003
3. Africana Studies and Research Center at Cornell University. January, 2013
4. The Journal of Blacks in Higher Education 2013 Report on Graduation Rates. January 1, 2013
5. 2013 Census Report on Income and Poverty in the United States. September, 2013.
6. The Pew Research Center Report on Wealth and Inequality. 2013. December, 2014.
7. The Pew Research Center Report on Views of Race and Inequality, Blacks and Whites Are Worlds Apart. June16, 2016

Chapter 2
Poverty

"A nation spending more money on military defense than social uplift is approaching a spiritual doom" [1]
-Dr. Martin L. King

Some fifty years ago, President Lyndon B. Johnson declared "War on Poverty" making poverty in America one of his top priorities during his tenure, not only raising awareness of poverty in black, brown, and white communities. While at the same time ensuring that government programs, including head start, and food stamps would help reduce poverty and assist America's poor. History reminds us that Dr. Martin L. King spent the last few years of his life working his Poor Peoples' campaign, which he hoped would force our government and the American public to acknowledge and resolve the problem of poverty for people of all races and backgrounds in the United States. Despite his great intention to raise the awareness of poverty, some fifty years after Dr. Martin L. King's economic dream, poverty not only continues to be the cancer that threatens our society but remains a significant factor in the advancement of many black and brown communities.

According to Clayborne Carson, Director of the Martin Luther King, Jr. Research and Education Institute at Stanford University *"King's dreams of economic justice remain unrealized, but not because they are impossible to achieve. "It is easier to celebrate King as a civil rights leader, because that was the easier part of his vision to realize,"* Carson said. *"The southern Jim Crow system was a regional anachronism rather than a national problem - the gulf between rich and poor - that we still prefer to ignore."* [2] One of the most promising hopes of Dr. King was the equal opportunity for blacks to share in the nation's economic prosperity; his transition from civil rights to human rights reminded us of his commitment towards equality for all American citizens, despite what racial background we belong to. As Dr. King reminded us in his I Have a Dream Speech *"the promise that all men would be guaranteed the inalienable rights of life, liberty, and the pursuit of happiness. It is obvious today that America has defaulted on this promissory note insofar as her citizens of color are concerned. Instead of honoring this sacred obligation, America has given the Negro people a bad check which has come back marked "insufficient funds." But we refuse to believe that the bank of justice is bankrupt. We refuse to believe that there are insufficient funds in the great vaults of opportunity of this nation."* [3]

Less than a month before his assassination, King spoke of unemployment statistics that belied the long-term unemployment in the black community, explaining that employment was not the ticket out of poverty. He revisited this point in a number of similar speeches in the months before and after. *"The problem of unemployment is not the only problem,"* King said. *"There is a problem of underemployment, and there are thousands and thousands, I would say millions of people in the Negro community who are poverty-stricken not because they are not working, but because they receive wages so low that they cannot begin to function in the main stream of the economic life of our nation. Most of the poverty-stricken people of America are persons who are working every day, and they end up getting part-time wages for full-time work."* [4] Some fifty years after the march on Washington, African-Americans and other minority groups lag far behind their white counterparts in enjoying the American Economic Pie. Despite closing of various economic gaps, disparities continue to plague many of the ethnic groups who often claim that they are excluded from receiving many of the nation's economic benefits due to systematic racism and exclusion.

Poverty in the 1960's:
The Civil Rights Movement challenged the United States to look at the issue of poverty. During the presidency of both JF Kennedy and LB Johnson; their administration initiated federal economic programs to address inequality, employment creation, and closing the economic gaps for all Americans. Following the assassination of JF Kennedy, President Lyndon B. Johnson transitioned into office and thereupon declared an *"unconditional war on poverty in America."* Poverty in America in the 1960's remained the prominent political debate between the Civil Rights Movement and the political satire of the Johnson's administration, Dr. King's poor people campaign and the War on Poverty movement defined the race, class and political strife of a nation emerging out of racial tensions, and struggling for an identity based on class.

According to Federal Poverty statistics in 1959, according to federal poverty statistics, at least 20.8% of families lived in poverty, while 16.5% of white families lived below the poverty line, 54.9% of black families were considered poor and fell below the federal threshold of poverty. One out of two female-headed households lived below the poverty line, two thirds of black female-headed households lived in poverty.[5] According to the institute for Research on Poverty, despite making strides in eliminating America's improvised population, African-Americans still remains disproportionately higher on the spectrum than any other ethnic groups in America. Poverty and income inequality remain persistent within American society and the world at large. Since the 1960', policymakers and scholars have understood that discrimination and poverty function as major barriers to opportunity in America. Though the United States has moved steadily towards elevating tolerance and equality, African-Americans, Latinos, and Native Americans have disproportionately lower incomes rates than any other ethnic or racial groups. Further these groups have disproportionately higher unemployment and poverty rates than their white counterparts. It is critical that Americans and the wider world continue to evaluate the state of civil rights, including consideration of income inequality and economic opportunity.[6]

During a speech at Stanford University in 1967, one year before his assassination, Dr. Martin Luther King, Jr. said, *"there are literally two Americas. One America is beautiful... overflowing with the milk of prosperity and the honey of opportunity.* "*But tragically and unfortunately, there is another America. This other America has a daily ugliness about it that constantly transforms the ebullience of hope into the fatigue of despair. In this America millions of work-starved men walk the streets daily in search for jobs that do not exist. In this America millions of people find themselves living in rat-infested, vermin-filled slums. In this America people are poor by the millions. They find themselves perishing on a lonely island of poverty in the midst of a vast ocean of material prosperity."* [7] There are several factors that account for the continued poverty in African-American communities, none more important than racism and in the 21st century legalized, and systematic exclusion from the American Dream.

While the Civil Rights Movement paved the way to increase the racial awareness of black poverty in America, it did not solve America's racial problem nor did not close the gap between the races. The movement did however spearhead dialogue of the rough inequalities that plagued our society, a society where African-Americans were always at the bottom. Figure 1 shows the poverty trend within a 50 year timetable. Though we have made substantial increases in closing the poverty gap, the data consistently shows that African-Americans still remain far behind any other ethnic group in the progression of economic gap. This graph also displays the poverty rate among the races during the Civil Rights Movement and through the economic prosperity of the 21st Century. See Figure 1 Below

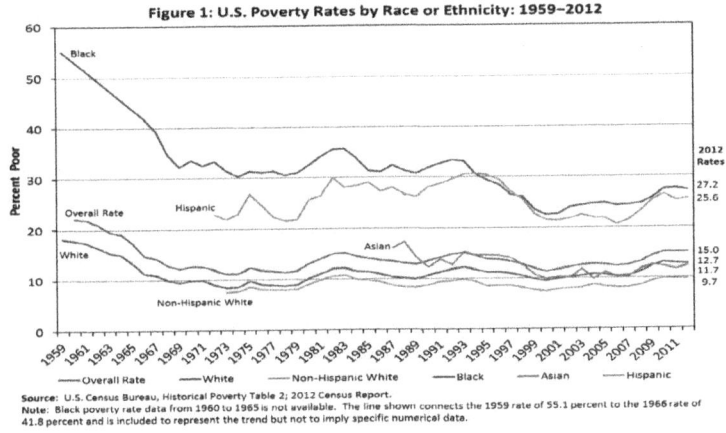

Source: US Census Bureau 2012 Report:

This data shows the drastic reduction in white poverty rates from 17% to 9.4% in 1979. The charts also shows is that while black poverty rates fell from a horrendous 55% in 1959 to just under 30% in 1979, it still remains the highest at 30% in 2010. It's important to note that black poverty rates remain three times that of whites, and comparatively are just as high as they were in 1959. Despite astonishing achievement in racial equalities in the 21s century, the wealth gap among the races continues to grow at an alarming rate.

According the 2011 US Census Bureau Report on Poverty in America, the poverty rate for all African-Americans increased from 25.5% in 2005 to 28.1% in 201. The report also indicated that the poverty rates increased between 2005 and 2011 for every demographic of African American families with children under 18, headed by a single mother. This demographic has the highest rate of poverty at 46.5% compared to only 8.6% percent of black families run by married couple.[8] In a 2013 Census report, the numbers still had not improved among the races. The nation continues to see a sharp racial divide in the incidence of poverty. In 2012, the Census Bureau reported that the poverty rate was 27.2 percent among blacks and 25.6 percent among Hispanics. For non-Hispanic whites, the 2012 poverty rate was 9.7 percent. For Asians, it was 11.7 percent.[9] Though we can all agree that the poverty rates have all decreased among the races since the 1960's, the persistent gap among the ethnic races continue to escalate at alarming rates. African-Americans and Hispanics as a result of their continued exclusion from many of the economic opportunities are still faced with the uphill task of climbing the economic ladder.

It is estimated that it will take both ethnic groups over 100 years to catch their white counterparts. Blacks and Hispanics still typically earn far less than whites, in part because whites dominate higher-paying fields this income gap has held fairly steady for the past 40 years.

See Figure 2 below.

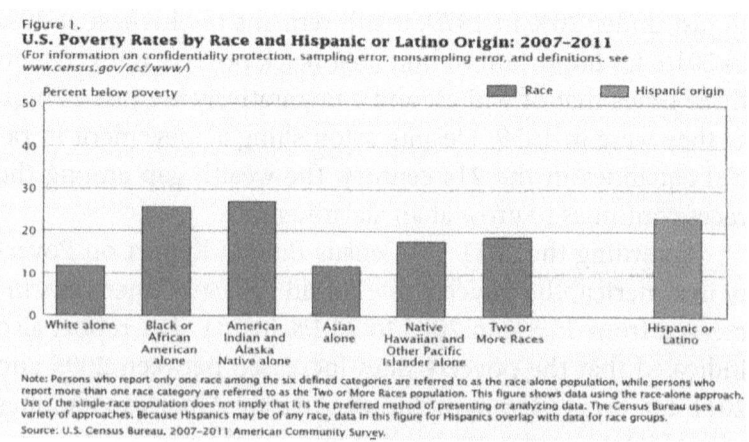

Source: US Census Bureau Report 2007-2011:

According to the New York Times article *"No racial or ethnic group experienced significant changes in income, but that left the gap between Asians, at the top, and blacks, at the bottom, as wide as before"*. The median income for Asian households was $68,600. For non-Hispanic whites, it was about $57,000, while the typical Hispanic household had an income of $39,000. The average income of a black household peaked at $33,300.[10] While income has increased in the last 40 years, African-Americans still lag far behind other ethnic groups with regard to economic empowerment. According to a new Pew Research Center analysis of data from the Federal Reserve, the wealth of white households was 13 times the median wealth of black households in 2013, compared to eight times the wealth in 2010, according to a new Pew Research Center analysis of data from the Federal Reserve.

Figure 3 below.

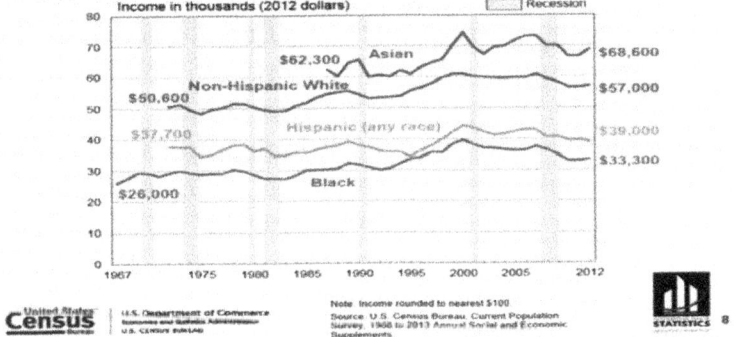

Source: US Department of Commerce Report 1967-2012.

According to a study by Shapiro and Sullivan *(The Racial Wealth Gap Increases Fourfold.)* between 1984 and 2007, the wealth gap between whites and blacks nationally increased fourfold from $20,000 to $95,000.[11] In 2007, the average white family had 20 times the wealth of the average black family.

While the Great Recession amplified the gap, much of the income disparity was due to intergenerational wealth through inheritance, social networks, the down payment on a home, the ability to pay for college tuition, etc.

- According to a November 2011 report by the non-profit organization, Feeding America, which includes a nationwide network of some 200 food banks, one in five of America's children are at risk of not having enough nutritious food to eat. For Hispanic and African-American children, the statistic is one in three.
- According to the Census data, the prevalence of poverty is higher for minorities–27.4% of African-Americans, for Latinos, the figure was 26.6%, and for Asians it was 12.1 percent. Roughly 10% of whites lived beneath the poverty line.
- Poverty is generally defined as earning $22,314 per year for a family of four. A person working 40 hours per week at the federal minimum wage of $7.25 per hour earns $15,080 per year, gross. According to the National Association of Child Care Resource and Referral Agencies, childcare alone can cost anywhere from $3,582 to $18,773 per year. [12]
- Using the official federal definition, 15.1% of the population is living in poverty – 46.2 million people. Using a supplemental measure that takes into account the geographical differences in cost of living, the number rises to 16%. [13]

The emergence of a small but powerful, and successful, black middle class that has enjoyed the fruits of its hard work and investments, like its white counterparts, must be acknowledged. Despite this amazing class mobility, African-Americans continue to fall far behind the other races. According to the Urban Institute, a non-partisan research organization, blacks have poverty rates almost three times as high as whites. Even more disturbing is the poverty rate among young African-Americans. According to the 2012 Census Bureau Report, over one-third of black children are living in poverty today (37.9%).[14] This is the highest of all racial groups, continuing this sharp upward trend along the poverty lines in America and over the past 25 years, reports show that the wealth gap between blacks and whites has nearly tripled.

U.S. Poverty Statistics–Age of the Population:

The child Poverty Rate is 21.1%, which equals more than one in five children are living in poverty status. This statistics is disturbing to many Americans because children are helpless to influence their living conditions. Many of these children come from single parent families as shown below. In fact, reports have suggested that many young African American children are living in economic conditions equivalent to that of third world countries.

Figure 4 below.

FIGURE 6

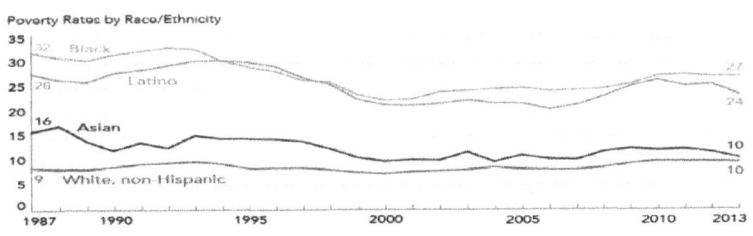

Source: U.S. Poverty Statistics 2014 Report.

As a measure of frustration on government policies towards to poor, Dr. King spoke out against government's war policies in Vietnam at the expense of the poverty in America. His poor people's campaign led to holding America accountable for its promise. *"We ought to come in mule carts, in old trucks, any kind of transportation people can get their hands on,"* he said. *"People ought to come to Washington, sit down if necessary in the middle of the street and say, 'we are here; we are poor; we don't have any money; you have made us this way ... and we've come to stay until you do something about it."* [15] Whatever the arguments maybe, there is a direct connection to race, racism, exclusion and our economic system and as a result many ethnic groups are exclude from the American economic pie.

According to the Pew Research Center report in 2014 on Child Poverty, they concluded that "overall, 20% of children in the U.S., or 14.7 million, lived in poverty in 2013–down from 22%, or 16.3 million, in 2010. (Poverty in 2013 was defined as living in a household with an annual income below $23,624 for a family of four with two related children.) During this period, the poverty rate declined for Hispanic, white and Asian children. Among black children, however, the rate held steady at about 38%. Black children were almost four times as likely as white or Asian children to be living in poverty in 2013, and significantly more likely than Hispanic children." The report also concluded that "In fact, the number of impoverished white children (4.1 million) may have dipped below the number of impoverished black children (4.2 million) for the first time since the U.S. Census began collecting this data in 1974, though this difference was not statistically significant. This is despite the fact that there are more than three times as many white children as black children living in the U.S. today.

Federal government data shows that African-Americans on average are at least twice as likely as whites to be poor or to be unemployed, homes headed by African-Americans earn on average little more than half of what the average white households earns. The underlying issue remains that race continues to play an important role in all public policy implementation. The fact of the matter is that economic disparities continue to exist in a nation that remains in debt with wars, useless foreign policies and economic aid. Racial disparities present a daunting challenge for people of color in the 21st century.

Figure 5 below.

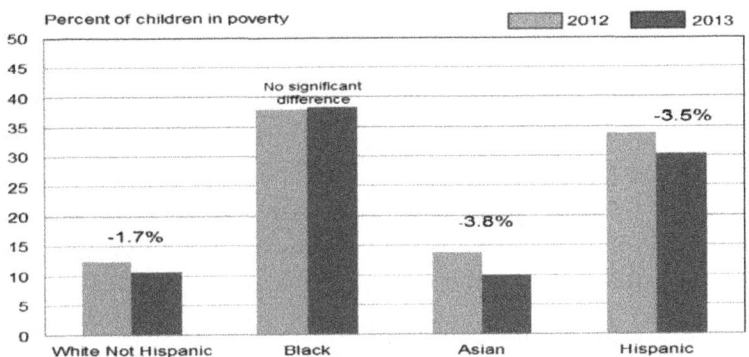

Source: US Census Bureau Report on Income and Poverty 2013.

Economic mobility is the primary factor that not only defines many African-American communities, but America as a whole. It has stripped us of the ability to see the best possible version of ourselves, as a nation and it has taken away the best of what we can become as a nation. Yes, race remains an important factor in many of our social ills, but correcting race with economic empowerment that is so urgently needed in many of our inner city communities.

Poverty: State of Connecticut: The Tale of Two States:

The State of Connecticut is often referred to as the gem of America as a result of its prosperity and long standing title of the nation's wealthiest state. Despite this accolade, Connecticut also houses three of the poorest cities in the nation. According to the federal government, while Connecticut continues to lead the nation in personal income, it also holds the dubious distinction of being No. 1 in the uneven distribution of wealth between the very rich and everyone else. According to the federal study, Connecticut had the largest gaps between the average incomes of the top 1 percent and the average incomes of the bottom 99 percent. Wealth and poverty are highly concentrated in Connecticut. Twenty-Seven percent of top-earning households live in neighborhoods that are predominantly white and wealthy, while lower income residents are likely to live in an extremely poor, predominantly minority filled neighborhoods. Three of the nations' poorest cities; Hartford, New Haven and Bridgeport which are also deemed black or brown cities, are plagued with economic disfranchisement, lack of opportunities and access to upward mobility for minority groups. Connecticut's larger cities are often referred to a "black or brown" cities due the large minority population that occupy these areas. These cities have the highest rates of poverty, despite being located in the wealthiest state. See Figure 6.

	White	Black	other	Hispanic
Connecticut	79.9%	9.4%	10.6%	12.0%
Bridgeport	48.5%	34.8%	16.7%	34.2%
Hartford	32.3%	37.4%	30.3%	41.3%
New Britain	73.4%	11.5%	15.1%	32.6%
New Haven	44.2%	36.1%	19.6%	24.3%
New London	61.8%	16.8%	21.4%	25.8%
Norwich	71.6%	11.7%	16.7%	8.0%
Stamford	64.9%	13.2%	21.9%	23.2%
Waterbury	64.1%	17.6%	18.3%	29.0%

Source: U.S. Census Bureau. 2011-2013 American Community Survey.

The information is depicted in Figure 6 below, shows that the poverty rates among peoples of color remain almost 3 times higher than their white counterparts. According to data produced by the Kaiser Family Foundation and the U.S. Census Bureau, African-Americans and Hispanics living in Connecticut are three times more likely to be poor than Whites. (A family of four is considered poor if their 2012 annual income is below $23,040, the federal poverty threshold.) Seven percent of Whites, 19 percent of Blacks and 25 percent of Hispanics are poor in Connecticut.[16] These numbers correlate the history or exclusion, oppression and systematic racism that are faced in many of these communities who are often excluded from the American dream.

See Figure 7.

Poverty Rates by Race/Ethnicity in Connecticut in 2011

	Persons with income less than Federal Poverty Level
Whites- non-Hispanic	7%
African-Americans	19.9%
Hispanic	25.3%

Source. Data from the U.S. Census American Community Survey (ACS) 2011 report.

Poverty hits African-Americans and Hispanics harder than most racial groups. Nearly 21 percent of African-Americans and 26.5 percent of Hispanics in Connecticut are embedded in poverty. These statistics can be attributed to a number of factors, including but not limited to access to economic opportunities, legal and systematic racism, cultural stereotypes, and white flight. Which has dismantled the economic base of many of Connecticut's' largest cities. Also mass migration of middle-class families in the 1960s, 70s, and 80s has left Connecticut's largest cities both economically and racially isolated. As a result, many peoples are stranded in the viscous culture of poverty. As of 2010, there were more than 720,000 people living at or near poverty line in Connecticut. This means that is almost 21% of all of state's population who are either currently living in poverty or facing the uncertainty of falling into poverty due to unemployment or under-employment.

According to an article in the Hartford Courant's article, Connecticut's poor regardless of race believe that the government is less responsive to residents' needs; that they have less access to goods and services, have less faith in police, have fewer chances to obtain suitable employment, have a lesser opinion of the condition of public parks and facilities; play less of a role in government decision making; show less tendency to remain in their communities long-term; believe that their neighborhoods are less safe; have less trust of their neighbors;

lack positive role models; are more likely to be in poor health; enjoy less overall life satisfaction; experience less happiness and more anxiety; and have higher rates of obese and overweight residents, and have lower rates of health insurance.[17] According to CT Junkie "The 50th anniversary of Lyndon Johnson's *"War on Poverty"* was five decades ago, but it wasn't until last week that the U.S. Census released data confirming that little progress has been made. While the report does not address how various anti-poverty programs have helped individuals and families over the years, it does provide an analysis of the rate of poverty overall. U.S. Census data found that poverty in Connecticut, which was around 9.6 percent in 1959, climbed to about 10.7 percent in 2013. That's the same place is was in 2012. The biggest increase in poverty was between 2003 and 2009 when it jumped from 8.1 percent to 9.4 percent." [18]

According the US Census report almost 365,000 people in Connecticut live below the poverty level, about 10.5 percent of the state population, or one in 10 state residents still live in poverty. The report also shows what most scholars for years have been reporting, that African Americans and Latinos are living at a higher rate of poverty than other groups, almost 21 percent of African Americans and 26.5 percent of Latinos in Connecticut are deemed poor by the federal government standards. Figure 8 below shows the growth of poverty in major inner cities in Connecticut.

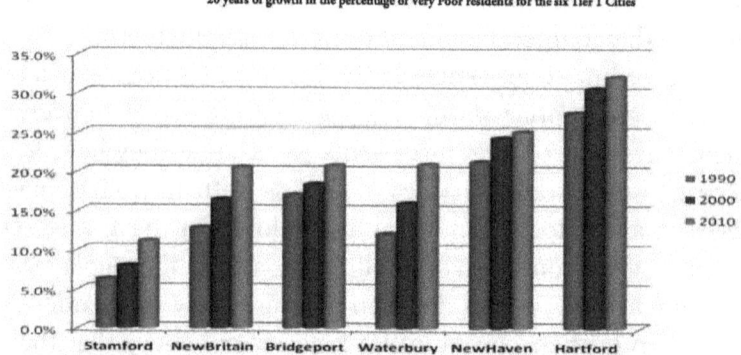

Source: US Census Bureau and Poverty in Connecticut. 2010.

According to the report, some of Connecticut's largest cities estimates of poverty rates varied significantly across the state: Bridgeport (25.7%), Danbury (13.9%), Hartford (36.0%), New Britain (25.5%), New Haven (30.1%), Norwalk (8.0%), Stamford (11.1%), and Waterbury (21.5%). The percentage of children under 18 living in poverty in Connecticut cities was also reported for Bridgeport (39.9%), Danbury (17.9 %), Hartford (47.9%), New Britain (35.7%), New Haven (41.4%), Norwalk (7.7%), Stamford (17.5%), and Waterbury (34.5%). Poverty estimates are only available at this time for cities with populations over 65,000. [19]

Connecticut cities depicted above have faced what most of America's cities have faced over the last 40 years, economic and racial strife. Since President Lyndon Johnson's declaration of War on Poverty and the passage of the Economic Opportunity Act of 1964, optimism that had surrounded those measures has faded. The economic, fiscal, and social conditions of the old central cities have declined, while their inner-ghetto areas have become zones of calamity. Their residents are not only living in poverty, but they must also contend with levels of drug use and violence that, although currently in decline, would have seemed inconceivable in the early 1960s.[20] Economic decay has also hit many of Connecticut's famous industrial cities. During the 1980's, Hartford's historically inexhaustible commodity, work, also began to vanish. Between 1980 and 1990, the city lost more than a quarter of its factory jobs. In the 1990's, Hartford's bedrock asset, its insurance industry, was decimated when 25,000 well-paid, high-skill jobs were cut, consolidated or conveyed out of town. Insurance remains central to the local economy.[21]

This element along with racial divisions, white flight, isolation of peoples of color and other raced based public policies have left many of these cities struggling to secure their rightful chance at Connecticut's economic pie. Of these elements, white flight was the threshold that led Connecticut cities in a disastrous position with little to no promise of building any racial alliances with its white sub-urban towns. In a state that holds a Caucasian population of roughly 83 percent white population, Hartford, Bridgeport, New Haven and New London eventually became an osmosis of poverty and people of color in the midst of an affluent state. One of best kept secrets in Connecticut's racial isolation is the element of child poverty in the richest state. According to the report, in 2014, 14.9 percent of Connecticut children lived under the 2014 federal poverty threshold of $24,008 for a family of four. That figure does not represent a statistically significant change from the figure from 2013. Over the same period, the national child poverty rate fell from 22.2 percent to 21.7 percent, a change which is statistically significant. In Connecticut, the median household income rose from $67,944 to $70,048 over the period, and the overall uninsured rate fell from 9.4 percent to 6.9 percent, mirroring national trends attributable to post-recession bounce-back and the introduction of the Affordable Care Act.[22] The report also identified a divide between racial and ethnic groups. In 2014, black and Hispanic children in Connecticut were more than five times as likely to live in poverty as white children. Hispanic children were more than twice as likely as white children to be uninsured, with black children only slightly more likely to be insured than Hispanic children.[23]

Among the races poverty has a great divide, African-Americans and Hispanics still hold the greatest gap as oppose to their white counterparts. According to the Census Bureau, 21 percent of African-Americans and 26.5 percent of Hispanics in Connecticut are poor. The numbers are worse for children with 30.5 percent of African-American children and 33.4 percent of Latino children in Connecticut living below the poverty line. The data below shows how that rates of overall and child poverty in Connecticut differs by race and ethnicity: African-Americans and Hispanic residents saw significantly higher poverty rates (20.8% and 26.5%, respectively) than white residents (6.1%) in 2014. The disparity was even greater, with rates higher for black children (30.5%) and Hispanic children (33.5%) than white4 children (5.6%) in 2014.[24] In fact, various reports have suggested that many young children of color in Connecticut are living in economic conditions equivalent to that of third world countries.

Figure 9. Child Poverty in Connecticut.

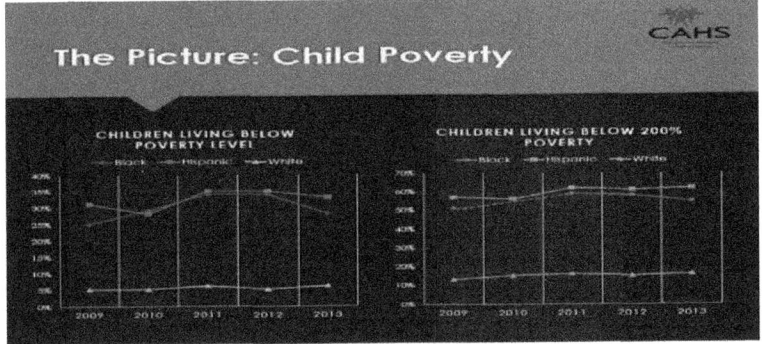

Source: Annie Casey Foundation Report 2013.

The report above shows that there are 13,000 more children across the state lived in low-income families in 2013 compared to 2008, during the recession. Twenty-nine percent of the state's children were part of families in which no parent had full-time employment, a 17-percent increase from 2008. It also concluded that there is still a divide between racial and ethnic groups. In 2014, black and Hispanic children in Connecticut were more than five times as likely to live in poverty as white children. Hispanic children were more than twice as likely as white children to be uninsured, with black children only slightly more likely to be insured than Hispanic children.

Conclusion:

Race continues to be a factor in the economic empowerment of the ethnic races in the 21st century, legalized and systematic discrimination and access to economic opportunities both continue to hamper the dream of economic prosperity among the nation's minority groups. Class disparities remains an important element that define many black and brown inner cities. When compared to the lack of upward economic mobility opportunities, this can be easily use to gauge the success of many African-American communities. These economic and class disparities permeates our society in ways that most do not realize, and plays a significant role in the frustration that plague many inner city urban communities, that African-Americans call home. This access to upward economic mobility is more important today than in any other time in our history and will be the key to bridging many of America's socio-economic and racial dilemmas.

Economic mobility is the driving force that defines many African American communities, and has continued to define who we are as Americans. It has often taken away the best of what we can become as a nation. Yes, race remains a key factor in many of our social ills, but correcting race must start with the economic empowerment that is so deeply needed in many of the inner city communities. Isn't what this country is all about: Achieving the American Dream for all?

References:
1. http://www.consortiumnews.com/2011/011611a.html
2. http://inamerica.blogs.cnn.com/2012/01/16/kings-final-message-poverty-is-a-civil-rights-battle/
3. I Have A Dream Speech. August 28th 1963.)
4. http://inamerica.blogs.cnn.com/2012/01/16/kings-final-message-poverty-is-a-civil-rights-battle/
5. http://povertyinamerica.mit.edu/download/atlas_of_poverty_in_america_p1.pdf
6. https://www.globalcitizen.org/en/content/the-civil-rights-movement-and-its-connection-to-po/
7. http://billmoyers.com/2013/04/05/two-americas-then-and-now/
8. (US Census Bureau 2011 Poverty Report, 2011.)
9. Ibid
10. NYT: Household Incomes Remain Flat Despite Improving Economy, September 17, 2013
11. (The Racial Wealth Gap Increases Fourfold.)
12. National Association of Child Care Resource and Referral Agencies
13. http://inamerica.blogs.cnn.com/2012/01/16/kings-final-message-poverty-is-a-civil-rights-battle/
14. The 2012 Census Bureau Report
15. http://www.newyorker.com/business/currency/race-and-poverty-fifty-years-after-the-march
16. The Henry J. Kaiser Family Foundation. Statehealthfacts.org. Poverty Rates by Race/Ethnicity, States (2009-2010), U.S.
17. http://www.courant.com/data-desk/hc-survey-wellbeing-changes-with-income-education-race-20160304-htmlstory.html
18. http://www.ctnewsjunkie.com/archives/entry/connecticuts_poverty_rate_remains_stubbornly_high/
19. http://www.ctvoices.org/sites/default/files/econ12censuspovertyacsrelsum2.pdf
20. https://www.huduser.gov/Periodicals/CITYSCPE/VOL-3NUM3/article3.pdf

21. http://www.nytimes.com/2002/08/26/nyregion/poverty-in-a-land-of-plenty-can-hartford-ever-recover.html?pagewanted=all
22. http://yaledailynews.com/blog/2015/10/01/child-poverty-rate-stagnates-in-connecticut/
23. Ibid
24. http://www.ctvoices.org/sites/default/files/econ15acscensuspovinc.pdf

Chapter 3
Black Lives Matter

"This is something that is deeply rooted in our society, it's deeply rooted in our history." adding, "When you're dealing with something as deeply rooted as racism or bias in any society you've got to have vigilance but you have to recognize that it's going to take some time, and you just have to be steady so you don't give up when we don't get all the way there." [1]
-President Barack Obama

Continued racial events have taken away the basic foundation of what our democracy stands for; life, liberty and the pursue of happiness, which is guaranteed to all who live in this promise land. The recent race based tragic events has only reminded us that there is need for a more constructive, and open dialogue on America's social cancer; RACE. This social cancer needs to be address in a very cautious but sensitive way in which all Americans can have a constructive meaningful dialogue but at the same time have a more proactive resolution. This dialogue must take place throughout all avenues of society, not only when a racial event stirs up racial hatred in our nation. This racial hatred leads to a racially sensitive nation in the short term and lost in the dialogue is the long term solution to America's problem that has been around for the last 300 years. Post racial America has been our foremost American dream with the elections of the nation's first African-American president.

The notion of leaving our racial hatred past of the 50's, and 60's have been always met with great expectations and optimism. This dream that America would transcend race and that racial attitude would undergo a fundamental change, despite this dream, it has not materialized in the 21st century. Events in Ferguson, New York City, Baltimore, and Charleston, SC have only reinforced the immense racial hatred and distrust in the African-American communities by white America. This dream that we are living in a post racial society where all are guarantee the benefits of our democracy has been lost in translation and dialogue about our continued racial reconciliation remains a silent debate unless another racial events stirs our nation's conscious.

The need for America to have a more constructive dialogue has not come to fruition for several factors, first, any discussion of race among white Americans illicit a very cautious and complicated reaction; many of whom often shy away from any constructive dialogue. Second, admitting we have a problem; a nation that is in denial and is sleepwalking will never wake up, and thirdly, many Americans refuse to acknowledge that racism is a societal problem which can be only resolved by having more open dialogue on race and discussion on diversity in America. Racial hatred continues to permeate our society in ways we don't even realize and it has continue to define who we are and what we stand for as nation that leads the free world and preaches democracy.

Recent race based events throughout the nation have once again left us scrambling for a solution to America's race problem, not only the earthshaking events of violence, destruction and disregard for human life but more so the frustration in many African-American communities. The riots take us back to the 1960s when many African-Americans were frustrated with the economic, social and political disenfranchisement of their American Dream. Yes, RACE was a factor but not the main underlying source of the frustration in many African-American communities. Baltimore and other poor cities has become the flagship of many poor urban communities, the a lack of economic mobility and community policing and a presence of poverty, drugs, deviant behavior, a failed education system and continued police brutality have continued to plague many inner-city African-American communities. Yes, race was a catalyst but not the underlying factor of these riots. The national debate that should be taking place is not what threat African-Americans pose to police and society but more so how we can correct a history of exclusion, oppression, legal and systematic racism against a community that remains loyal to a country that treated them as outsiders.

Race and race riots have taken away the best of who we are as Americans and what we can become as a society. The idea of Americans living in a post-racial society where all races are guaranteed the benefits of the American Dream and a society where race and racism no longer exists have almost disappeared in many urban minority communities.[2] Thus, there lies the problem among many poor urban cities, these issues compounded with excessive police distrust and frustration has led to many of the urban riots we encounter today.

The failure to have a constructive dialogue on many of the urban issues that affect many African-American communities is the underlying cause of the frustration among many inner-city urban dwellers. The lack of modern-day policing techniques, community involvement, communication but more so trust and faith in police fuels much of the debates that should be taking place today. Historical racism between police forces and African-Americans throughout the country has led to climate of distrust, hate and disregard for black lives that has fueled much of the frustration that is being depicted today. Baltimore matters because American lives matters; the recent events have only reinforced that race continues to define who we are as Americans and perpetuate the fact that we are still not living in a post-racial era. These events have taken away the best of who we are as Americans and what we can become as a nation. These recent earth-shaking events throughout the country have left us gasping for a solution for America's problem. Only conversations about the truth, the need for reconciliation, America's acknowledgment of its past wrongdoings, and access to economic opportunities for all can lead to a more racially-tolerant society. These riots have only reinforced that white and black racial attitudes have not undergone a fundamental change and race continues to be a catalyst that fuels much of the debates that are taking place today.

Baltimore and other black and brown cities should not be held as the scapegoat for America's socioeconomic, political and race-based problems, but it should be held as a leader for the national dialogue that should be taking place. Baltimore represents much of what is to be black in America, frustration among America's urban dwellers, poor socio-economic conditions that has led to this dilemma of anger and frustration among its residents. There needs to be a national discussion that should not be taking place only in black and brown cities but throughout the nation on America's social ills. Evaluating the series of constant protest throughout the country at times violent, but mostly non-violent has left a deep uncertainty on the role rage, race and rebellion that continue to plague many African-American communities. These events continue to voice the frustration of upward economic mobility, social despair, disregard for black lives, police brutality and many other social ills that many African-American communities are embedded in.

The recent riots only addressed police brutality but gone from the discussion that should be taking place are the continued economic class warfare that has plagued many of these inner city communities. The access to upward economic mobility in many African-American communities is the underlying cause of their frustration that has manifested itself into a race rebellions and riots. The discussion that America must address is how we increase upward economic mobility in a community that has been denied their rightful piece of the American pie. Gone from the dialogue is the upward economic mobility and its impact on the riots, gone from the dialogue is the continued social oppression that plague these inner cities, gone from the dialogue is why are many African-Americans and their communities continue to plague with economic starvation and poverty? These frustrations played an important role in many of the riots in the 1960's which was often labeled race riots and not class rebellions. The social uprising were part of the economic warfare and disparities that haunted many African-American communities, yes race was a factor in the 1960's but not the main underlying source of the frustration found in many African-American communities.

In the 21st century there are still many facets of oppression that exist and are prevalent in many African-American communities, silent and not overt racism exists in their school systems, employment, poverty, healthcare, prison system, and other sectors of their societies.[3] Class disparities continue to be an important element that define many black and brown inner cities and compelled with the lack of upward economic mobility opportunities this can be easily use to gauge many African-American communities. These economic and class disparities permeates our society in ways we don't even realize and plays an important role in the frustration that plague many inner city urban communities that African-Americans call home. This access to upward economic mobility is more important today than in any other time in our history and will be the key to bridging many of America's socio-economic and racial dilemmas.

The idea of Americans living in a post-racial society where all races are guaranteed the socio-economic benefits of the American dream and a society where race and racism no longer exists have almost disappeared in many African-American communities. African-Americans and other minority groups remain one of the most underrepresented communities in schools, the workforce and other sectors in American society due to a direct result of economic racism, class discrimination, and more so their exclusion from the American pie. Whatever the arguments are, there is a direct connection to race, and racism, our economic system, and the underlying issue remains that race continues to play an important part in all public policy implementation. Economic mobility is the main factor that continues to define many African-American communities and has continued to define who we are as Americans and has often taken away the best of what we can become as a nation. Yes, race remains an important factor in many of our social ills, but correcting race must start with the economic empowerment that is so deeply needed in many of the inner-city communities.

Recent race riots throughout the country has left many questions that continue to haunt our society: community policing, trust in law enforcement, but more so the continuing significance of race in America. The recent riots that surrounded the death of Michael Brown and others have continued to open the debates about the discussions on race, criminal justice, and America's post racial society. Unfortunately this debate has neither materialized nor even blossomed and any discussion on race takes away the best of who we are as Americans. Whether we admit it or not, racism continues to be a significant factor that haunts our great country as we delved into the deep waters of race in America. The race riots in many black and brown cities can be traced to economic, social and racial factors that continue to haunt many poor African-American communities, distrust in policing, stereotypes of young black males but more the failure to talk about race and the acknowledgment that race still plays an important role in our society. The riots brought many debates to the forefront of America, that's in the 21st century oppression continue to exits and are prevalent in American society.

A recent poll suggested that there is deep divide on the black lives matter movement, according the latest New York Times poll, *"Black and white opinion is sharply divided on the aims and the approach of the Black Lives Matter movement. Seventy percent of African-Americans are sympathetic to the movement, compared with only 37 percent of whites. Among all Americans, 41 percent agree with the movement, 25 percent disagree and 29 percent do not have an opinion either way."* [4] In fact the new Civil Rights movement *"Black Lives Matter"* seem to be more generational than objective according to the responses by Americans. The same New York Times Poll finds that *"Support for Black Lives Matter correlates directly to age, with 50 percent of all adults younger than 30 saying they agree with the movement, compared with 20 percent who disagree with it. Among those 45 and older, 36 percent agree and 29 percent disagree."* [5] The response among the races also indicate that we are still a divided nation when it comes to race relations, the poll showed that *"Black and white opinion is sharply divided on the aims and the approach of the Black Lives Matter movement. Seventy percent of African-Americans are sympathetic to the movement, compared with only 37 percent of whites. Among all Americans, 41 percent agree with the movement, 25 percent disagree and 29 percent do not have an opinion either way."* [6]

See Figure 1.

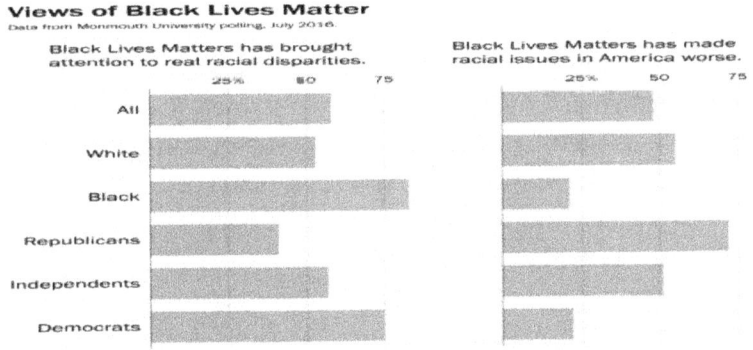

Source: Monmouth University. July 2016

The above report by Monmouth University shows the continued racial attitudes and differences on the new Civil Rights Movement that has arisen due to continued racial abuses against African-Americans.

Michael Brown's death, along with other African-Americans, race riots and peaceful social protest has become another part of the puzzle why race matters in America. The fact that many Americans refuse to come to terms that the history of the African-Americans is a struggle against racism and oppression in a country that still today refuses to acknowledge and apologize for its actions and wrongdoing. As a result, lack of discussion of race among law enforcement, community engagement organizations, and white Americans fuels our greatest enemy. Any discussions of race among white Americans leaves a very cautious and complicated reaction, many of which often shy away from any constructive dialogue. The race riots have brought many factors to the forefront, none more important that the fact we need to acknowledge that race and racism is a societal problem which can be only resolved by having more open dialogue on race and discussion of diversity in America. Only conversations about the truth, the need for reconciliation and America's acknowledgment of its wrong doing can lead to a more racially tolerant country where the American dream can be enjoyed by all despite race or color.

The stereotypes of young black males continue to be a major disappointment in society, Michael Brown and other deaths became another element that defines our racial perception of who black men are. The famed termed *"Can't Legislate Morality,"* coined by the late Arizona senator and presidential candidate Barry Goldwater, remains a message that is lost in today's society, and reminiscent of what happen in Ferguson, MO and many black and brown cities. According to Senator Goldwater in 1964, despite the passage of many Civil Rights laws, it's still imbedded in our conscious to discriminate against African-Americans and other minority groups. The idea that Michael Brown, a young black male might be a threat to law enforcement a thug and just an outright deviant member of society reinforces the racial stereotype on how we view young black men and race in America. Michael Brown's death fuels the debate on what happened to the idea that America would become a melting pot that we are constantly reminded of and often embrace. His death reminds us that this melting pot did not melt and it remains a distant dream. The fact is that the failure to talk about race and racism, and the failure to acknowledge that racism exist in the 21st century, is what fuels one of the most debatable topics in America. The events like Ferguson, MO, and other parts of America constantly remind us that we have a long way to go to achieve a post racial society and a melting pot that is sought after in America.

We as a nation must critically evaluate the legacy of the Civil Rights Movement, which primarily fought for the advancement of opportunities of African-Americans, guaranteeing their constitutional rights, eradicating legalized and systematic racism in Jim Crow south but more so making America a more racially tolerant society. Have we forgotten this dream? Have we forgotten the message of hope, the foundations of our democracy? Are we as a nation suffering from amnesia? It's time to wake up reflect our wrongdoing, social ills and make a conscious effort to move forward as a country and as a people despite what color we are. America is still two nations: one White and one Black. There needs to be a national discussion that should not be taking place only in Baltimore but throughout the nation on America's social ills.

The dialogue must include different races, police, community activist, political leaders, clergy and any other members of inner urban communities. Only conversations about the truth, the need for reconciliation, and America's acknowledgment of its wrong doing can lead to a more tolerant society where the American dream can be enjoyed by all. Black lives matter, because American lives matter.

References:

1. http://www.breitbart.com/video/2014/12/07/obama-racism-deeply-rooted-in-us/
2. http://www.huffingtonpost.com/stephen-balkaran/post-racial-america-in-th_b_6954332.html
3. http://www.ijessnet.com/wp-content/uploads/2015/02/9.pdf
4. http://www.nytimes.com/2016/07/14/us/most-americans-hold-grim-view-of-race-relations-poll-finds.html?_r=1
5. Ibid
6. Ibid

Chapter 4
Education

"The question as to whether American Negroes were capable of education was no longer a debatable one in 1876. The whole problem was simply one of opportunity." [1]
-W.E.B. DuBois, 1935

The landmark Supreme Court case of Brown v. Board of Education (1935) brought an end to any laws that established racial school segregation, by deeming those laws unconstitutional and having no place in America society. Education equality remains the pinnacle of debates well into the 21st century, as we seek to analyze the success of Brown and equal education for all Americans. In regards to education equality, Chief Justice Earl Warren, on behalf of the U.S. Supreme Court, declared, *"In the field of public education, the doctrine of 'separate but equal' has no place. Separate educational facilities are inherently unequal."* Dr. Martin Luther King, Jr. aptly described this decision as a *"joyous daybreak to end the long night of enforced segregation."* Also, the decision made in Brown v. Board of Education overturned the 1896 ruling on Plessy v. Ferguson, which upheld the state laws requiring racial segregation as long as the facilities were 'separate but equal.' The Brown decision was supposed to end segregation within the public schools, and ultimately led to the destruction of racial discrimination in other areas of American life, but clearly in the 21st century this is not the case.

The <u>Brown v. Board of Education</u> decision was a combination of five different cases that went before the Supreme Court. This case was named for Linda Brown, a third-grader in Topeka, Kansas, who was forced to travel more than an hour each day to an all-black elementary school, rather than attend the all-white school located just blocks from her home. The landmark case ended with the Supreme Court establishing that all state laws that had created separate public schools for African-American and white students were unconstitutional. Some sixty-years after the <u>Brown v. Board of Education</u> decision, the question of how far we've come in eliminating segregated education in America is still relevant. Since 1954, the Civil Rights Movement has fought diligently to dismantle racial discrimination in America's public schools, yet despite this historic case, the struggle for equality continues to be a goal that has left our nation grasping for a solution. More than sixty-years after <u>Brown vs. Board of Education</u>, our school system in the United States continues to be separate and remains unequal. The idea of an integrated education society, where all colors can become one and enjoy the benefits of this great nation, remains lost and continues to be embedded into the notion of race based education.

According to Beverly Tomek, *"education was an important component of the Civil Rights movement"* for a number of reasons. First, blacks were denied the right to vote throughout the South by means of literacy tests. Thus, it was important to teach southern blacks the basics of literacy so they could pass the tests and gain political power through the franchise. Also, despite orders to desegregate public schools, blacks throughout the South remained in second-class facilities. They were provided with outdated, worn-out books and materials, and taught by teachers who were under social and economic pressures to teach them to accept the prevailing social order. This situation hurt students' self-esteem and left them feeling trapped by the system. Finally, the segregated nature of the schools perpetuated racial division. The only way to break this hold was to work outside the official educational structure and bring in teachers who would not only show students that education could empower them to better their lot, but who would show them that blacks and whites could work together to transcend the existing social order and achieve unity from the bottom up.[2] The issue of school desegregation has been one of the foremost issues of the Civil Rights agenda. The former notion *"separate but equal"* was built on notions of white supremacy, which provided legal justification for "Jim Crow" laws that required separate accommodations for whites and blacks in many U.S. states and cities, laws that continued right into the 1960s.

The Dilemma:
Despite the legalized eradication of school segregation, Harvard University's Civil Rights Project reported that schools today are more segregated than they were in the past. The report shows that U.S. schools are becoming more segregated in all regions for both African-American and Hispanics students. The Civil Rights Project reported that *"we are celebrating a victory over segregation at a time when schools across the nation are becoming increasingly segregated."* [4] According to The Civil Rights Project at UCLA, some fifty-years after the March on Washington, and sixty years after the Brown decision, not only do 76% of African-Americans attend segregated schools, but *"Across the country, 43 percent of Hispanics and 38 percent of blacks attend schools where fewer than 10 percent of their classmates are whites."* The Project also reported that more than one in seven black and Latino students attend schools where less than one percent of their classmates are white. According to a New York Times article by N.R. Kleinfield, in the 2009-10 school year half of New York City public schools were 90 percent black and Hispanic. Progress has been limited since

the days of the Little Rock Nine and the quality of education depends on the zip code with which you live; white suburban students remain ever more isolated from interactions with students of other races and classes.[5]

Segregation of Latino students is most pronounced in states like California, New York, and Texas. The most segregated cities for blacks include Atlanta, Chicago, Detroit, Houston, Philadelphia, and Washington, D.C. Professor Gary Orfield, Director of the Civil Rights Project, indicated that *"Extreme segregation is becoming more common."* Recent research by USA Today shows that the segregation of Hispanics from white communities across the USA has declined significantly for every Hispanic group except the largest: Mexicans. According to a report from the US 2010 project, which researched changes in American society, Mexicans make up 60% of the nation's more than 50 million Hispanics, and are so prevalent they drown-out distinct characteristics of non-Mexicans.

According to Professors Feagin and Barnett, *"however, that despite the positive effects in education and other areas resulting from the Court's Brown decision, the decision has by no means been successful in dismantling institutionalized racism in American education. They note that although schools may be officially desegregated, they nevertheless remain effectively segregated due to the following: discrimination in schools by administrators, teachers, and students; racial bias in school curriculum; the separation of students into different ability tracks reflecting racial, class, and gender stratification; and the use of standardized testing that contains significant racial and class bias."* [6] Continued de-facto segregation has remained imbedded in American culture. As a result, in the 21st century, education has remained separate and unequal, and students of color continue to receive sub-par education.

Author Gene A. Budig's educational achievement, *"No simple answers to racial inequality"* (2010), is important not only unto itself, but also because it directly relates to levels of health, employment, income, and civic engagement. Average public high school graduation rates are 83% for whites, 66.1% for blacks, and 71.4% for Hispanics. Low-income, Hispanic, and African-American students are more likely to need remediation than their wealthier, white peers (41% of Hispanic students and 42% of African-American students require remediation, compared to 31% of white students).[7] In their recent report on the <u>Brown</u> decision, The National Assessment of Educational Progress (NAEP) shows that black fourth-graders now average higher math scores than the average white math scores only a generation ago. Yet because average white achievement has also improved, the gap between black and white achievements remains. The average black student still performs better than only about 25 percent of white students, making the goal of equal qualification for the labor market a distant and daunting goal.

According to MSNBC's Education Racial Gap, the academic performance of the nation's twelfth graders in math and reading has not changed since 2009. According to the National Assessment of Educational Progress, which on Wednesday released The Nation's Report Card on America's high school seniors, the white-black gap in math and reading scores in 2013 was 30 points, the latter of which grew five points since 1992. The White-Hispanic gap was 21 points in math and 22 points in reading. For more than a decade, many state and federal policies have attempted to narrow the achievement gap, but the gulf between whites and their black and Hispanic counterparts has remained steady or, in some instances, widened. Though we have made progress in closing many of the gaps that plague black and brown education facilities, the disparity among the races remains an alarming signal that achieving equality through education and advancing the nation's Civil Rights agenda remains lost in translation in the 21st century.

See Figure 1. National High School Assessment Scores; Math and Reading.

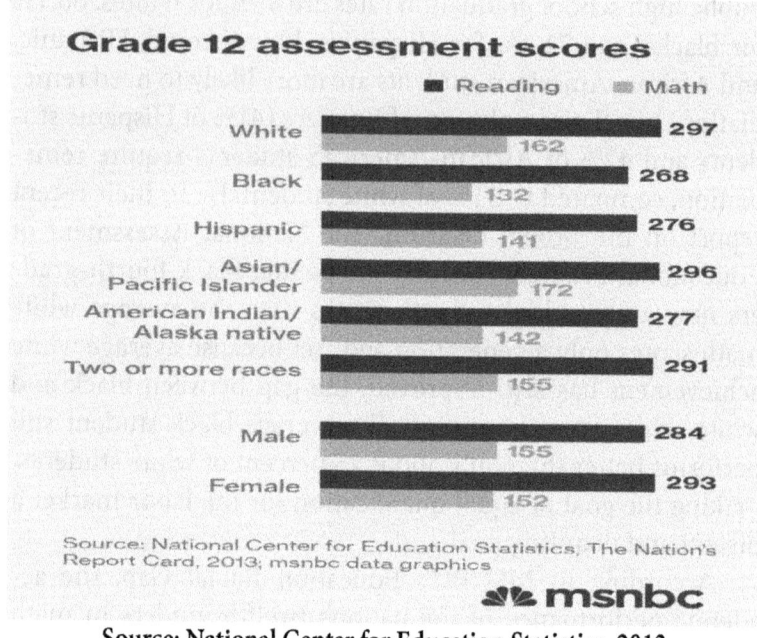

Source: National Center for Education Statistics. 2013

At the collegiate level, the percentage of 25 to 29 year-olds who have a bachelor's degree is 39% for whites, 20% for blacks, and 13% for Hispanics. The above study also indicates that the National Assessment of Student Progress score gaps between blacks and whites in mathematics and reading have not changed in twenty years. Schools are becoming more segregated: approximately 4% of black and Hispanic students attend high schools that are more than 90% minority, up from less than a third in 1988." [8] According to the Pew Research Center, in 2014, 35% of Hispanics ages 18 to 24 were enrolled in a two- or four-year college, up from 22% in 1993 – a 13-percentage-point increase. That amounted to 2.3 million Hispanic college students in 2014.

By comparison, college enrollment during this time among blacks (33% in 2014) increased by 8 percentage points,

and among whites (42% in 2014) the share increased 5 points. (Pew Research Center report 2016 Races and Education)
See Figure 2.

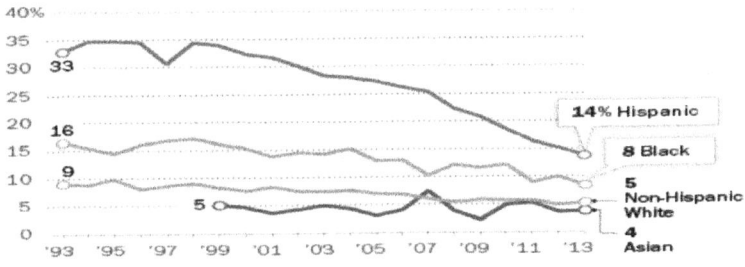

Source: Pew Research Center report 2016 Races and Education:

When it comes to college graduation rates, Whites, African-Americans, Asian-Americans, and Hispanic-Americans are all graduating from colleges and universities at higher rates now than previous generations, yet we can still see that racial gaps are widening among the masses. According to the federal data, between 1995 and 2015 the percentage of white 25-29-year-olds attaining bachelor's degrees has risen from 29 to 43 percent, a gain of 14 percentage points. Among blacks, the percentage with bachelor's degrees has gone up by six only six points, from 15 to 21 percent, and for Hispanics it has risen seven points, from 9 to 16 percent. According to Kimberlee Eberle-Sudre, Ed Trust Policy Analyst *"We caution institutional leaders who celebrate their graduation rate gains to take a good look at their data and ask whether they are doing enough to get more African American, Latino, and Native students to graduation and to close completion gaps."* [9] "The answer for many institutions is, 'No.' Fewer than half of the institutions we analyzed raised rates for their underrepresented students *and* cut gaps.

Figure 3.

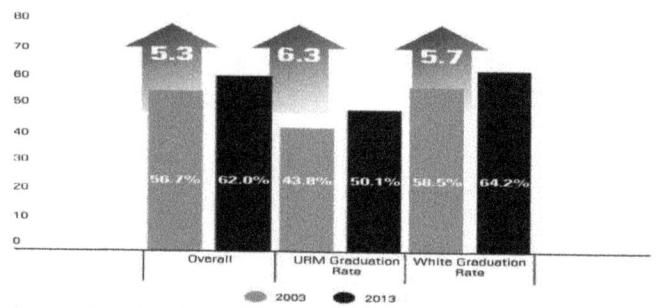

Source: Ed Trust Report College Graduation Rates. 2015:

Though this may be a small, yet promising, gain, the report argues that we are not even close to closing the fourteen-point collegiate graduation gap. At this pace, we will not close this gap this century, for the national graduation rate for white students in 2013 alone was 64 percent, compared with 50 percent for minority students.

The continued racial inequality in educational opportunities can be attributed to a number of factors: (1) Underperforming, poorly financed schools characterized by low quality of teaching, large class sizes, and inadequate facilities that perpetuate underachievement by minority students; (2) School assignment policies that promote segregation; (3) School district boundaries that are coterminous with town boundaries and local land use, zoning, and taxation powers; (4) Systems of ability grouping and tracking that consistently retain or place minority students in lower level classes with less exposure to curriculum that builds critical analytical skills; (5) failure to counteract differences in parental income and educational attainment factors that impact a child's development and which often correlate with race; and (6) Lower teacher and administrator expectations of minority students *(Racial Disparities in Educational Opportunities in the United States. By John Brittain & Callie Kozlak. Seattle Journal of Science. Spring 2008).* Furthermore, the issue of race, racism, and education is exacerbated by white flight and de-facto racial segregation. In fact, according to Brittain and Kozlok's *"Racial isolation and school segregation are increasing in the United States,"* education for white, black, and brown students depends on the zip code with which you live.

Today, the average white child attends a school where 77 percent of the other students are white. The average black student attends a high school where only 30 percent of the other students are white. For example, in New York State, 60 percent of all black students, including those in New York City, attend schools that are at least 90 percent black. Nationally, 76 percent of Hispanics attend predominantly minority schools.[10] Increased segregation is problematic because racially-segregated, minority schools tend to have dramatically fewer resources and employ less experienced teachers. Disparate educational resources lead to larger class sizes, substandard facilities, lower per pupil spending, and fewer counseling services. Furthermore, *"segregated minority schools are more likely to be housed in high-poverty neighborhoods that have high crime rates and limited access to community resources that enhance learning and development."* [11]

According to Catharine Lahmon, Assistant Secretary for Civil Rights, U.S. Department of Education, we have not fulfilled the Brown Promise of equal education, *"We have come far, but we obviously have not come far enough. And that's the depressing reality that I think has to light a fire under all of us. It certainly lights a fire under me in the work that I do. And we need to be working to deliver on that promise."* [12] In "How, after 60 years, Brown v. Board of Education succeeded- and didn't," the Washington Post concluded the following observation that addressed the short comings of the landmark decision.

- Although Brown stimulated a Civil Rights movement that desegregated many facets of American society, it was least successful in integrating education, the decision's aim.
- Initial school integration gains following Brown stalled and black children are more racially and socioeconomically isolated today than at any time since data have been available (1970).
- Academic achievement of African-Americans has improved dramatically in recent decades, but whites' has as well, so racial achievement gaps remain huge.
- Schools for black children had enormous resource shortages in 1954. Inequalities still exist in some places, although they are much smaller. But resource equality itself is insufficient; disadvantaged students require much greater resources than middle-class white students to prepare for success in school.
- Expensive but necessary resources include high-quality early childhood programs, from birth to school entry; high-quality after-school and summer programs; full-service school health clinics; more skilled teachers; and smaller classes.
- Even with these added resources, students can rarely be successful in racially and economically isolated schools where remediation and discipline supplant regular instruction, excessive student mobility disrupts learning, involvement of more-educated parents is absent, and students lack adult and peer models of educational success.
- Schools remain segregated today because neighborhoods in which they are located are segregated. Raising achievement of low-income black children requires residential integration, from which school integration can follow. Education policy is housing policy.
- Federal requirements that communities must pursue residential integration have been unenforced, and federal programs to subsidize movement of low-income families to

middle-class communities have been weak and ineffective.
- Correcting these policy shortcomings is essential if the promise of Brown is to be fulfilled.[13]

Sixty-years later, school segregation is still a problem and continue to be a policy that is engulfed in race based decisions. The majority of black and brown students continue to attend schools where they are the majority. While Brown did end legal segregation and brought much of the society's hidden racism into the public, the law did not address de-facto segregation. Economic segregation, racial isolation, white flight, and continued racism have led to more segregated schools than the 1950's.

Although students of color in America have made a number of educational advancements since <u>Brown v. Board of Education</u>, the decision did not succeed in dismantling school segregation with deliberate speed as depicted in the court's decision. The implementation of <u>Brown v. Board of Education</u> remains one of the most disappointing public policies in America's Civil Rights history, and continues to perpetuate why race and racism still matters in America. Correcting this public policy and education have taken so many twists and turns that it has become a more racially motivated policy which has done more harm than correcting one of America's greatest social ills: Education

State of Connecticut: A Case Study:

Despite the opportunity to attend integrated schools and colleges, African-American and Hispanics students still lag behind all other ethnic groups in Connecticut graduation rates. The implementation of the <u>Brown v. Board of Education</u> decision remains one of the major failures in the struggle for equality in America. The majority of minority students continue to attend school districts where they make up the majority, often in areas where the school system is sub-par to their white counterparts.

The racial apartheid education system in Connecticut continues to haunt our society and remains the major element as to why disparities continue to exist in the 21st century. In 1989, the city of Hartford, CT challenged the <u>Brown v Board</u> decision in a lawsuit *(Sheff v O'Neil)* claiming that segregation still existed in Hartford public schools. In 1996, the Connecticut Supreme Court ruled in favor of the plaintiffs and ordered the State of Connecticut to take the remedial measures necessary to integrate schools. Despite this historic ruling in Connecticut, *"Hartford-area schools remain divided by race and class. Though inter-district magnet schools and other programs have given some of the region's children access to quality, integrated educational opportunities, fewer than one in 10 Hartford-resident students of color attends an integrated school."* [14] Despite all of the challenges faced in the past, the issue of racial discrimination can still be found in schools across the state.

When comparing the tale of two Connecticut cities, Bridgeport and Greenwich are the two perfect examples of the inequality of wealth and poverty, and of black and white. *"The distance between these two places is not much, about 20 miles, but the gulf that separates them often seems too great to navigate for many residents on both sides of the divide. The vastly different experience of growing up in either cannot be exaggerated. Bridgeport, with its dilapidated factories and graffiti-scarred public housing projects, is a world away from the half-dozen other affluent communities that line the Connecticut shoreline between them, such as Westport and New Canaan."* [15] Despite being in the same county (Fairfield) the affluent atmosphere of Greenwich surpasses all other towns. Immense in wealth from Wall Street, hedge funds, investment banking, and private equity groups nestled in the downtown business districts, Greenwich's community is centered on private affluent country clubs, mansions, and private and public schools that have the highest test scores, graduation rates, and college acceptance rates in Connecticut. Bridgeport, on the other hand, continues to be plagued by poverty, violence, dilapidated housing, drug infested communities and high dropout rates, similar to most of Connecticut's inner cities.

The Achievement Gap is often depicted as the performance of poor and minority students in comparison to the performance of white students in the state standardized exams. In fact, Connecticut leads the nation when it comes to the achievement gap between white-suburban and inner city-black and brown test scores. According to research conducted by the Connecticut Association for Human Services, schools in high poverty areas, such as Bridgeport, perform much worse on standardized tests than schools in wealthy areas, such as Fairfield. The Fairfield School District experiences high achievement scores across the board in all subjects as compared to the rest of the state of Connecticut. See Figure 4 below.

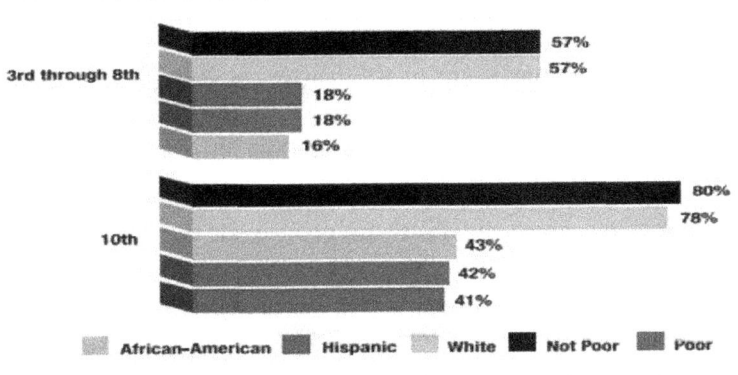

Source: Connecticut CVNT Report. 2010.

The data above shows the continued, alarming gap among the races and economic class. Connecticut has the worst white-minority achievement gap in the nation in math and reading and, according to the results of other major tests given, not much has changed since the *Sheff v. O'Neil* case in Hartford in 1989.

According to the report "Opportunity in Connecticut: The Impact of Race, Poverty and Education on Family Economic Success," given the changing demographics of our state, it is imperative that we work now to improve the educational and economic outcomes of all Connecticut children. Data shows that a gap related to access and success exists among students at each point in their educational careers, from preschool enrollment to the number of two- and four-year college students who lack fundamental reading, writing, and math skills. Connecticut's children of color, and those from low-income and poor families, are disproportionately on the low end of the state's academic achievement gap.

Connecticut's notoriety as having the largest gap in the country based on race-ethnicity and socioeconomic status is illustrated in the two graphs below depicting fourth-grade math score gaps and eighth-grade reading score gaps among White, Black, and Hispanic students. According to State of Connecticut Department of Education, post high school and college enrollment remains another widening gap among the ethnic races. The report concludes that "Enrollment in college during the first year after high school graduation varied considerably across racial/ethnic groups for the class of 2013. Asian students were the most likely to enroll (83.2 percent), followed by white students (77.7 percent), Native Hawaiian or Pacific Islanders (70.8 percent), Black or African American students (63.9 percent), multiracial students (69.6 percent), Hispanic/Latino students (59.2 percent), and American Indian or Native Alaskan students (58.5 percent)." (CDSE College Enrollment, Retention, and Graduation: Statewide Results Report 2013)

See Figure 5. Education Gap in Connecticut.

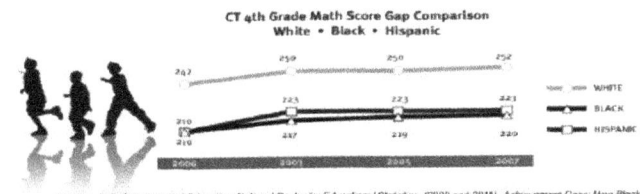

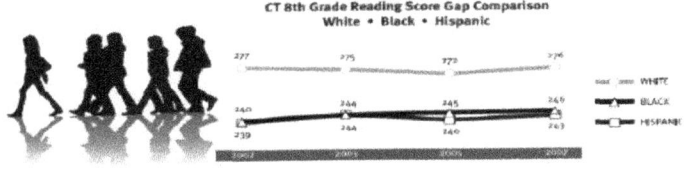

Source: U.S. Department of Education. National Center for Educational Statistics. (2009 and 2011).

The graduation rates among Whites, African-American, and Hispanics remains the largest achievement gap in the nation; students of color still remain at the bottom of the graduation table despite the integration of schools in the 21st century. The notion that "separate" was inherently unequal has remained an institutional part of our state's educational system. Predominantly inner city school systems that serve predominantly black and brown students remain under funded, have higher dropout rates, and produce lower test scores than predominantly white school systems. In a 2011 report titled Equity in Education: A Transformational Approach, researchers found that "*Connecticut's children remain highly segregated by race and income in its capital city, as well as across the state,*" some fifteen years after the landmark Sheff v. O'Neill case ordered Connecticut schools to correct racial gaps in education.

See Figure 6. CT High School graduation rates and Ethnic races.

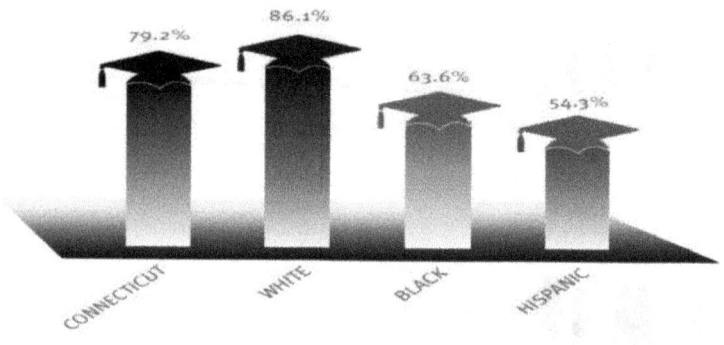

Source: Education Counts Graduation Rates. 2011 Report:

Despite the fact that schools are integrated across the country in the 21st century, the issue of racial segregation and the inequality of education remains a distant idea. This proves that there is no equal education system in the United States of America. While many Americans like to believe that the country has made great strides in education equality, it is a fact that we still have a two-fold system of education, one for whites and one for students of color.

A recent Connecticut's Superior court ruling ordered the State of Connecticut to re-evaluate its education policy and allocation of its resources. The decision vested changes in financing, evaluation, teacher's evaluation, curriculum and other elements that define the schools' districts, both rich and poor, black and white in Connecticut. Judge Thomas Moukawsher of State Superior Court in Hartford said that *"Connecticut is defaulting on its constitutional duty"* to give all children an adequate education.[16] According to the Judge *"The current system "has left rich school districts to flourish and poor school districts to flounder," betraying a promise in the State Constitution to give children a "fair opportunity for an elementary and secondary school education."* [17]

According to the Judge Moukawsher's decision, a state that as taunted its impressive education system including being nationally ranked has short-changed many poor districts, which serve mostly black and brown students. According to the ruling, Connecticut has some of *"the highest average reading scores in the country for fourth and eighth graders on the 2013 National Assessment of Education Progress, or N.A.E.P., often called the nation's report card. But the state is also home to failing schools, especially those serving poor children."* [18] The 2015 N.A.E.P. report also found that poor students in 40 other states, including perennial poorly performing Mississippi and Arkansas, did better than poor students in Connecticut. Interestingly the decision which affects many poor communities in Connecticut which are often labeled black or brown school communities, are often associated with minority students.

Conclusion:

Connecticut's education system has become the beacon for inequalities between the access white and minority students have to quality education. According to University of Arizona social scientist Lane Kenworthy, *"Inequality of opportunity has increased in recent decades," "[A]vailable compilations of test scores, years of schooling completed, occupations, and incomes of parents and their children strongly suggest that the opportunity gap, which was narrowing until the 1970s, is now widening."* Put simply, in today's America, the children of the rich will likely get richer; poor children will probably remain so, and those in the vast middle class will be challenged, even in two-income households, to just tread water. [19]

The Civil Rights issue of the 21st century: Education Disparities, and the State of Connecticut remain one of the most debated subjects. Why does the nation's wealthiest state have such a huge educational disparity among white-suburban, and inner city-black and brown students? Race and race based education still matters in Connecticut.

References:
1. http://northbysouth.kenyon.edu/1998/edu/home/web.htm
2. Education, Civil Rights, and the War on Poverty, Beverly Tomek
3. Harvard University' Civil Rights Project: School Segregation on the Rise despite Growing Diversity among School-Aged Children
4. The Civil Rights Project at UCLA- Deepening Segregation and Challenges
5. New York Times article: Why Don't We Have Any White Kids?
6. University of Illinois Law Review. 2004.
7. No simple answers to racial inequality. Gene Budig
8. Ibid
9. Kimberlee Eberle-Sudre, Ed Trust Report on Graduation Rates 2015
10. Brittain and Kozlok's "Racial isolation and school segregation are increasing in the United States.
11. Ibid
12. http://www.pbs.org/newshour/bb/60-years-brown-v-board-school-segregation-isnt-yet-american-history/
13. https://www.washingtonpost.com/news/answer-sheet/wp/2014/04/24/how-after-60-years-brown-v-board-of-education-succeeded-and-didnt/
14. https://www.aclu.org/cases/sheff-v-oneill
15. http://www.npr.org/2013/01/17/169509521/in-connecticut-two-sides-of-a-deep-economic-divide
16. http://www.nytimes.com/2016/09/08/nyregion/connecticut-public-schools-inequality-judge-orders.html?_r=0
17. Ibid
18. Ibid
19. http://www.npr.org/2013/01/17/169509521/in-connecticut-two-sides-of-a-deep-economic-divide

Chapter 5
Immigration

"Immigration Reform One of the Biggest Civil Rights Issues of Our Time." [1]
-Mark Zuckerberg. CEO of Facebook

No other time our country's great history has a debate on immigration divided the nation on its true value and rich tradition in welcoming immigrants with open arms. Not only had the debate gone into the presidential political spectrum it has become the Civil Rights issue that will define the future America. The political debacle of the current Civil Rights issue has left the United States of America divided along racial, ethnic and political lines, never seen before in our great country. The issue now revolves around whether Dr. Martin L. King would consider immigration a Civil Rights Issue? That question is answered in his famous quote *"I choose to give my life for those who have been left out ... This is the way I'm going. If it means suffering a little bit, I'm going that way.... If it means dying for them, I'm going that way."* Dr. Martin Luther King Jr., from "The Good Samaritan," 1966.[2]

The Comprehensive Immigration Reform policy is directly related to the future of America, both to the American people as to who we are, what we stand for, but more so to the political parties as they try to court America's greatest asset--The Hispanic Vote. Very few Americans understand the current Hispanic changing demographic trends, its implications, and its political importance.

This decision will ultimately define the future political landscape in America. The political importance of the Hispanic vote is closely tied to Immigration reform and, whether or not we admit it, the American presidency will be dictated by the Hispanic vote. The recent immigration laws in Arizona, Mississippi, Pennsylvania and other states have raised several important questions regarding to the role of the federal government's policies, Civil Rights, public policy decision making process and more so the role of race-Civil Rights in many of the decision making processes. The Immigration debate has now generated so many divisions in our society that it has become the *"Civil Rights debate of 21st century"*; never in American history has immigration become such a decisive issue where policymaking and the electoral process goes hand in hand.

The Hispanic presence in America dates back to the founding of this great nation, Hispanics have contributed in every avenue of American life since the inception of this great country. Many are unaware that Hispanic culture had firm roots in St Augustine, Florida and what is now New Mexico before the English arrived at Jamestown and before the Pilgrims dropped anchor in Massachusetts Bay.[3] Despite the contributions of immigrants, our history has reminded us that any ethnicity that sought home in America was faced with several acts of discrimination and hatred. Throughout our history the U.S. immigration policies of welcoming other groups have been tainted with race based policies, for example, The Naturalization Act of 1790, which granted the rights of American Citizenship to all "free white persons"; the Chinese Exclusion Act of 1882 barred Chinese immigrants from becoming naturalized citizens.

Benjamin Franklin in 1753 warned of German immigrants overrunning America, and not only was he concerned about the increasing number of German immigrants. He worried that the German immigrants would threaten the Anglo English language and insisted that America must set the principle of Anglo-conformity as the model of immigration. Samuel Huntington, who some argue was our first president under the Article of Confederation, once described brown skins Mexicans as savages and uncivilized. Interestingly, both gentlemen were signers of the Declaration of Independence, which preaches Life, Liberty and the purse of Happiness.

Moreover, the plight of immigrants and the discrimination faced by their communities in America ranges from hateful slurs to barring of their ships in U.S. ports pre and post holocaust years. Whatever the debates are, the issue of color now emerges to haunt the much debated role of race in the American society. From the time of the nation's founding, immigration has been crucial to the United States' growth, and also been the source of political and Civil Rights conflict.

The Hispanic Civil Rights debate goes far beyond the typical immigration debates on loss of jobs, drain on our social system, criminals etc., it has now vested on the *"Browning of America."* In recent decades, the country has experienced the second great wave of immigration which many argue the largest since our country's establishment. According to Mary Waters and Karl Eschbach's <u>Immigration and Ethnic and Racial Inequality in the United States</u>. *"The new global order has changed the racial and ethnic map of the United States one further way. Immigration has had a very large impact on American society since the 1960s, and most especially it has increased the diversity of the nonwhite population of the United States. In 1990, 7.9% of the US population was foreign born. The 19.8 million foreign-born people in the United States is the largest number in US history. The sources of immigration flows have also shifted as a consequence of changes in immigration law and in the international pattern of migration flows. In 1990, 25.2% of the foreign-born population was Asian, 42.5% Latin American, 22% European, and 10.3% from other countries."* [4]

Immigrants and immigration have played and will continue to

play an important role in our country's rich diverse culture yet that rich culture has been tested by the guarantee if one's Civil Rights. The economic, political and social clout of current immigrants and the immigration debate are far more beneficial to the nation than our critics point them out to be. Hispanics are fast becoming the new cornerstone of this country's economic, political and social power and based on their potential, no other immigrant group in the history of our great nation has the potential to redefine America and make us great.

President Donald J. Trump's racist remark reminds us that the hatred towards immigrants is alive and well in a country that preaches integration and acceptance of all. His remarks still remind us that there is still a need for vigilant Civil Rights enforcement. Very few Americans remember the historical racism that Mexican immigrants encountered in the early 1900's, then the U.S. Public Health Service (USPHS) in 1916 began implementing a series of anti-health laws targeted at Mexican immigrants crossing the U.S.–Mexico border. The US Health Department and our government rationale was that Mexicans were bringing diseases into the United States, therefore American health policies had to change in order to secure the border and keep Mexicans out of America. Another example of racist remarks and policy directed towards Mexican immigrants occurred in the 1929 stock market crash. This event led to the greatest depression in American history, a time when one out four Americans was unemployed, our economy shattered and confidence in American idealism was tested.

As many Americans suffered from the economic depression, Mexican immigrants became the scapegoat for America's economic, social, and political problems. As a result, Mexican immigrants were denied jobs, subjected to raids, illegally arrested and detained without due process. As a result of this fear of immigrants, the American government between 1929 to 1939 deported some one to two million Mexican American citizens and legal residents of Mexican descent; this mass deportation was known as the Mexican Repatriation policy with the aim of cleansing America's ill. Immigrants became the scapegoat for America's economic, social, political problems, these policies, along with other racist ideologies, continued to persist throughout the 1930's, 40's, 50's '60's and to the 21st century. According to Garcia, Ruben J., Critical Race Theory and Proposition 187: The Racial Politics of Immigration Law. *"Undocumented immigrants provide a convenient scapegoat for the social problems currently confronting America, making anti-immigrant rhetoric prevalent and acceptable in politics today."* [5]

The 2013 Comprehensive Immigration Reform policies are geared to the future of both political parties as they try to court America's greatest asset: The Hispanic Vote. The Immigration debate has generated so many divisions in society that it has become the Civil Rights debate of 21st Century. Never in American history has immigration become such a divisive issue where policymaking and the electoral process goes hand-in-hand. Moreover, how both parties handle the issue of comprehensive immigration reform will have a serious impact on Hispanic political behavior and future presidential elections. The 2013 Immigration Reform Bill deals with the following issues.

1. The economic effects of legalizing millions of currently illegal immigrants while also increasing the rate of future immigration.
2. The possibility of achieving real border security and
3. The ethical question of offering the reward of citizenship to those who entered the country illegally.

The growing presence of the Hispanic community will have profound political consequences and future immigration policy agendas will play an important part in the political process. Both parties have acknowledged the importance of the Hispanic vote and Immigration Reform, and they have approached the new voting sector more cautiously as the 2013 Immigration Reform Bill becomes a stumbling domestic policy for the potential presidential candidates. Very few candidates have addressed immigration reform with any constructive dialogue or solutions, and even those who have addressed immigration have doomed themselves to failure in the eyes of many Hispanics electorates. Their decision will ultimately lead to a backlash from their own constituents and those of favor or impede efforts to provide a path to citizenship for undocumented immigrants living in America. Since 2010 the number of Hispanic eligible voters has increased by some 3.9 million. Their share among eligible voters nationally is also on the rise, the 2014 elections, the Hispanic electorate accounted for 11% of total voters, up from 10.1% in 2010 and 8.6% in 2006, reflecting the relatively faster growth of the Hispanic electorate compared with other groups.[6]

According to Senator Lindsey Graham (R) *"If we don't pass immigration reform, if we don't get it off the table in a reasonable, practical way, it doesn't matter who you run in 2016. We're in a demographic death spiral as a party, and the only way we can get back in good graces with the Hispanic community, in my view, is pass comprehensive immigration reform."* [7] The Democratic Party argues, *"Hispanics are a swing vote; they are no longer a base vote of our party. Though we can all agree that it is the democratic agenda that will help Hispanics live a better life, we need to tell them in a compelling way. When we speak to them we can move them our way; they can break the Republican Party."* The Republican Party also acknowledged the political importance of the Hispanic vote, *"given the size, growth rate and the distribution of Hispanics, it is safe to say that if we do not respect their voting power, they can change the future of elections."* [8] Thus immigration reform has a greater long-term effect that many Americans have come to realize, how we approach the new Civil Rights issue must be done in a cautious and sensitive way in order to accommodate the socio-economic and political power in America.

The Dilemma:

The growth of the Hispanic electorate will be an important factor in an increasing number of congressional races across the country in upcoming elections and beyond. More numbers mean more votes. Their presence is now swing votes in some 14 states and can increase to 16 states by the Presidential election of 2016. According to the 2013 American Progress report on the Growth of Latino Electorate in Key states, they concluded that *"given the Latino population's rapid growth its political influence will be greater in 2016 elections, over the next 4 years the Latino voters nationwide is projected to increase by 4 million people-an increase by 17%. The Latino community's influence is even more pronounced at the state level and key states where the growth of Latino eligible voters is outpacing all other groups."* [9] This increased population growth along with immigration reform will bring more votes to the table, and how to attract these voters becomes a political chess game for both Democrats and Republicans. Moreover, how both parties handle the issue of comprehensive immigration reform will have a serious impact on Hispanic political voting behavior in 2016 Presidential and future elections. The growing presence of the Hispanic community will have profound political consequence on each political party and future immigration reform policy will play an important part in defining America's new political process and the struggle for equality.

If the Immigration Reform Bill were to pass, what would be the implications on our political landscape? The new law will allow unauthorized immigrants to gain eventual citizenship but also carries electoral risks and rewards for both Republican and Democratic Parties. On the one hand, if the bill were passed, its paves the way for new voters but more important which political party will they align themselves with? According to Nate Silver, *"roughly 80 percent of illegal immigrants are Hispanic, and about 10 percent are Asian, both groups that voted heavily Democratic in the last two elections. On the other hand, such legislation could plausibly improve the Republican Party's brand image among Hispanics and Asian-Americans, perhaps allowing the party to fare better among these voters in future elections."* [10] These immigration changes will have a long term effect on our political process: they would affect the status of the 11 million unauthorized immigrants who are already in the United States who will eventually become U.S. Citizens and exercise one of the fundamental rights we have in America; the right to vote.

According to the Congressional Budget Office, if the Immigration Reform Bill becomes law, it will add more than 17 million new potential voting-age citizens by 2036. These potential voters are in addition to the nearly 15 million that the current level of legal immigration will add by 2036. Combined, current immigration would add more than 32 million potential new voting-age citizens by 2036. [xi] These changing political demographics paint an alarming political fiasco that neither political party can afford to underestimate. If the bill becomes law, Hispanic youths and naturalized immigrants will be 34 percent of newly eligible voters in 2014, 35 percent in 2016, 36 percent in 2018, and 37 percent in 2020. [xii] California will experience the greatest impact of the Immigration Reform Bill, with nearly two-thirds of newly eligible voters belonging to either Hispanic or Asians. The same effect will take place in many other states where the voting power will be held by swing votes in both current and future elections. States like New Mexico, Texas, Florida, Virginia, North Carolina, Colorado, New York, New Jersey and Nevada will now have an important and decisive Hispanic vote that will dictate the future of elections, Civil Rights and political parties.

These immigration changes will have a long term effect on our political process: they would affect the status of the 11 million unauthorized immigrants who are already in the United States who will eventually become U.S. Citizens and exercise one of the fundamental rights we have in America; the right to vote. These changing political demographics paint an alarming political fiasco that neither political party can afford to underestimate. If the bill becomes law, Hispanic youths and naturalized immigrants will be 34 percent of newly eligible voters in 2014, 35 percent in 2016, 36 percent in 2018, and 37 percent in 2020. [11] Failure to deliver a sensible Comprehensive Immigration Reform Bill might spell death and allegiance of the Hispanic vote for both political parties in 2016 Presidential and future elections.

Both parties must be cautious and reflect on California's Proposition 187, an anti-immigrant policy which outlawed affirmative action and bilingual programs in the early 1990s and its long term effect on the Republican Party that sponsored the legislation. At a time when the Hispanic electoral was only 10% of the state population, this anti-immigrant policy began to mobilize California's Hispanic community, and by 2012 some 70% of Hispanics identified with the Democratic Party. Hispanics not only began taking part in the electoral process but voted heavily Democratic; this anti-immigrant policy awoke the sleeping giant in California---the Hispanic vote. California's political landscape was never the same and became heavily democratic as a result of Proposition 187 anti-immigrant policy directed towards Hispanics. Not only did the mobilization of the Hispanic vote in California destroy the relationship with the Republican Party, it cost them an important voting bloc for future elections.

Some 20 years after Proposition 187, Hispanics are California's largest voting bloc and the political representation in the state has since doubled among their legislators. Can this effect be a new national dilemma facing both Democrats and Republicans, can the Hispanic vote be closely tied the Immigration Reform Bill, can the future of both parties afford not to please the Hispanic swing votes? These questions rest solely on the importance of both political parties and how they court America's growing important swing votes. Neither political party can afford to play with the Hispanic vote; immigration reform is a key tool to courting America's greatest political asset. How both political parties resolve the immigration debacle can be an important gauge on the future of American political process, political activist, Presidential hopeful, and businessman Donald Trump remarked, *"Immigration reform is a suicide mission for GOP."* [12]

Conclusion:

Despite this socio-economic influence the debates are vested on the issue of race based policies rather than the rich great diverse culture Hispanics present to our great nation. How and when both political parties address immigration reform remains a struggle; there must be a common-sense ideology on immigration reform by both the Democratic and Republican parties. Immigration reform can have severe consequences on how American democracy is shape and define. There must be a sensible solution to the Civil Rights issue of the 21st century--immigration reform. Civil Rights which came about as a result of the 300 years' oppression of African-Americans and their struggle for equality and acceptance into American society today has paved the way for a new Civil Rights debate. Immigration Reform.

References:

1. http://abcnews.go.com/blogs/politics/2013/11/mark-zuckerberg-immigration-reform-one-of-the-biggest-civil-rights-issues-of-our-time/
2. Dr. Martin Luther King Jr., from "The Good Samaritan," 1966
3. What Would America be like without Hispanics
4. Mary Waters and Karl Eschbach's Immigration and Ethnic and Racial Inequality in the United States.
5. Garcia, Ruben J., Critical Race Theory and Proposition 187: The Racial Politics of Immigration Law
6. Latino Voters and the 2014 Midterm Elections, Geography, Close Races and Views of Social Issues By Mark Hugo Lopez, Jens Manuel Krogstad, Eileen Patten and Ana Gonzalez-Barrera.
7. Senator Lindsey Graham. NBC Meet the Press. June 8th 2103.
8. 2004 Presidential Race and Democratic Party
9. How Immigration Reform and Demographics Could Change Presidential Math By Nate Silver. April 30. 2013
10. Ibid
11. Stepping Up: The Impact of the Newest Immigrant, Asian, and Latino Voters by Rob Paral. Immigration Policy Center Report 2013
12. Donald Trump. Washington Times. March 15 2013

Chapter 6
Criminal Justice System

"Mass Incarceration in the Age of Colorblindness; we have not ended racial Caste in America, we have merely redesigned it, describing how Jim Crow laws and legal racial segregation have been replaced by mass incarceration, serving as "a stunningly comprehensive and well-designed system of racialized social control." [1]
-Michelle Alexander

One of America's best kept secrets is its race based criminal justice system. African-Americans and other peoples of color are disproportionately incarcerated, profiled, and sentenced at significantly higher rates than their white counterparts. Not only are people of color disproportionally incarcerated for the same crimes as whites, but minority communities in the 21st century are still plagued by the denial of their Civil and Voting Rights, the lack of access to college financial aid, and the lack of adequate job opportunities. In light of these race based disparities, it is imperative that criminal-justice reform evolves as a Civil Rights issue in the 21st century. According to <u>Racial and Ethnic Disparities in the US Criminal Justice System</u>, *"African-Americans make up 14% of the general US population, yet they constitute 28% of all arrests, 40% of all inmates held in prisons and jails, and 42% of the population on death row. In contrast, Whites make up 67% of the total US population and 70% of all arrests, yet only 40%*

of all inmates held in state prisons or local jails and 56% of the population on death row. Hispanics and Native Americans are also alarmingly overrepresented in the criminal justice system." [2]

African-Americans being abused by the industrial prison system is nothing new; in fact, it dates back to the height of the Jim Crow era in the 1890's when the prison gangs system coerced labor in the industrial south. As a result, African-American males were charged with fake crimes, sentenced to prison, and then sold into force labor: SLAVERY BY ANOTHER NAME. Additionally, according to Michelle Alexander's The New Jim Crow: Mass Incarceration in the Age of Colorblindness, more black men are incarcerated, on probation, or on parole than there were enslaved in 1850, before the Civil War began. Fast forward into the 21st century, African-Americans now constitute nearly 1.1 million of the total 2.3 million people incarcerated and are incarcerated at a rate nearly six times higher than whites. Together, African-Americans and Hispanics comprised 58% of all prisoners in 2011, even though they only comprised approximately one quarter of the US population. See Figure 1 below.

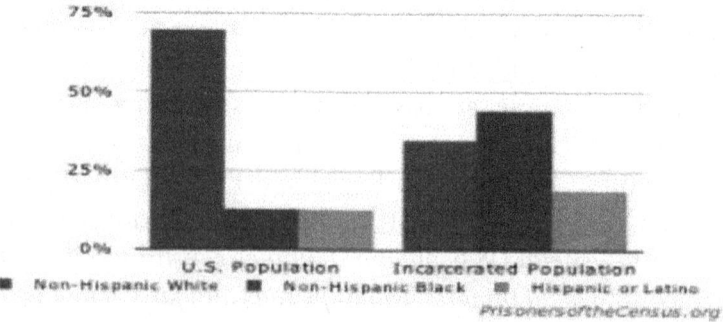

Source: Sentencing Project Report 2013.

While white Americans make-up 67 percent of the U.S. population, they only make-up 31 percent of the incarcerated population. In contrast, African-Americans represent 14 percent of society but 36 percent of prisoners. Similarly, Hispanics represent 16 percent of the U.S. population but 24 percent of the prison population.

According to the US Census Bureau in 2012, *"The Census estimates that approximately 18,508,926 people in the U.S. population are black males, of all ages...The Bureau of Justice Statistics' National Prisoner Statistics Program reports that in that same year, 526,000 were in state or federal prisons, and, as of mid-year 2013, 219,660 were in local jails, making for a total of about 745,000 behind bars"* [3] Figure 2 below shows that the United States incarcerates more African-American males than the entire prison population of India, Argentina, Lebanon, Canada, Germany, Japan, and England combined.

Figure 2.

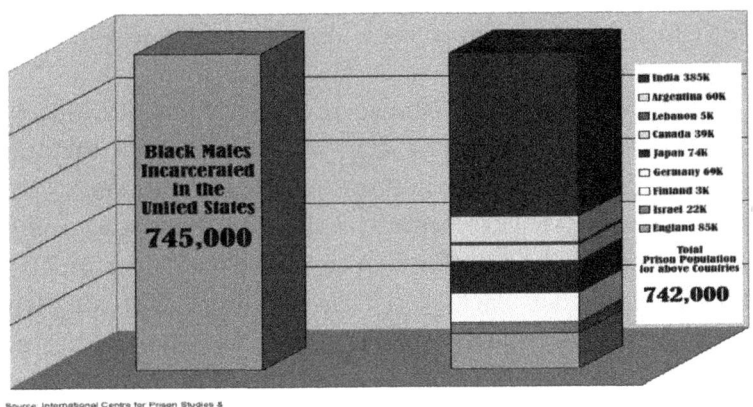

Source: Bureau of Justice report 2013.

In fact, due racial incarceration's business-like nature, prisons are now a $70-billion-dollar enterprise; it's profitable to keep people locked up.

According to the Sentencing Project's "Reducing Racial Disparity," *"So long as racism exists within society at large, it will be found within the criminal justice system. Racism fuels the overt bias which can show in the language, attitudes, conduct, assumptions, strategies and policies of criminal justice agencies. Instances of overt bias can lead in turn to the improper use of discretion among actors in the criminal justice system."*[4] Despite the fact that whites engage in drug offenses and criminal activities at a higher rate than African-Americans, African-Americans are incarcerated at a rate ten times greater than whites. The Center for American Progress outlines several facts about the criminal justice system, Civil Rights, and minority communities. They list as follows: (The Center for American Progress: A Look at the Racial Disparities Inherent in Our Nation's Criminal-Justice System. March 2012.)

1. While people of color make up about 30 percent of the United States' population, they account for 60 percent of those imprisoned. The prison population grew by 700 percent from 1970 to 2005, a rate that is outpacing crime and population rates. The incarceration rates disproportionately impact men of color: 1 in every 15 African-American men and 1 in every 36 Hispanic men are incarcerated in comparison to 1 in every 106 white men.

2. According to the Bureau of Justice Statistics, one in three black men can expect to go to prison in their lifetime. Individuals of color have a disproportionate number of encounters with law enforcement, indicating that racial profiling continues to be a problem. A report by the Department of Justice found that blacks and Hispanics were approximately three times more likely to be searched during a traffic stop than white motorists. African-Americans were twice as likely to be arrested and almost four times as likely to experience the use of force during encounters with the police.

3. Students of color face harsher punishments in school than their white peers, leading to a higher number of youth of color incarcerated. Black and Hispanic students represent more than 70 percent of those involved in school-related arrests or referrals to law enforcement. Currently, African-Americans make up two-fifths and Hispanics one-fifth of confined youth today.

4. According to recent data by the Department of Education, African-American students are arrested far more often

than their white classmates. The data showed that 96,000 students were arrested and 242,000 referred to law enforcement by schools during the 2009-10 school year. Of those students, black and Hispanic students made up more than 70 percent of arrested or referred students. Harsh school punishments, from suspensions to arrests, have led to high numbers of youth of color coming into contact with the juvenile-justice system at an earlier age.

5. Once convicted, black offenders receive longer sentences compared to white offenders. The U.S. Sentencing Commission stated that in the federal system black offenders receive sentences that are 10 percent longer than white offenders for the same crimes. The Sentencing Project reports that African-Americans are 21 percent more likely to receive mandatory minimum sentences than white defendants and are 20 percent more like to be sentenced to prison.

6. Voter laws that prohibit people with felony convictions to vote disproportionately impact men of color. An estimated 5.3 million Americans are denied the right to vote based on a past felony conviction. Felony disenfranchisement is exaggerated by racial disparities in the criminal-justice system, ultimately denying 13 percent of African-American men the right to vote. Felony-disenfranchisement policies have led to 11 states denying the right to vote to more than 10 per- cent of their African-American population.[5]

People generally agree that discrimination based on racial or ethnic origin is morally wrong and a violation of the principles of equality and justice. The equality principle requires that all people be treated equally based on their similarities; race should not be considered in that assessment *(May and Sharratt 1994: 317)*. America has a number of biases in its criminal justice system, and one can only conclude that race defines and rules our criminal justice system in the 21st century.

According to Michael Sclafani's <u>Civil Rights in Present Day America</u>, *"In the year 2010 there were 220,700 black in-*

dividuals that were incarcerated for some reason, compared to 38,000 white people during the same year." [6] These numbers are astounding when compared to the size of the African-American population in the country. People struggle to fathom the massive racial gap that exists in the number of people who are incarcerated each year. There are roughly 182,700 more blacks in prison than whites, which shows the African-American incarceration rate is exponentially higher than the white American incarceration rate. These statistics show that a major difference exists between the arrest and imprisonment of African-Americans and that of other races. Sclafani also concluded that if African-Americans and Hispanics were incarcerated at the same rate as whites, America's prison and jail populations would decline by approximately 50%.

Figure 3 below provides a national view of the concentration of prisoners by race and ethnicity as a proportion of their representation in the state's overall general population, or the rate per 100,000 residents. The chart displays that blacks are incarcerated at a rate of 1,408 per 100,000 while whites are incarcerated at a rate of 275 per 100,000. This statistic proves that blacks are incarcerated at a rate 5.1 times higher than whites. This national look also shows that Hispanics are held in state prisons at an average rate of 378 per 100,000, a disparity ratio of 1.4:1 compared to whites.

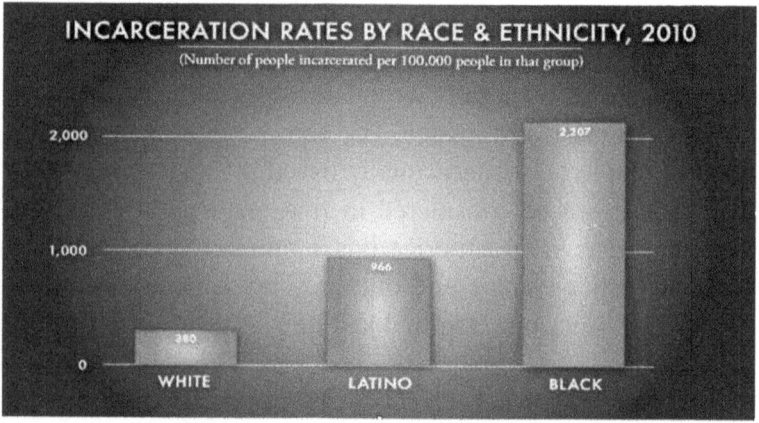

Source: Prison Policy Initiative 2010 Report.

According to the Sentencing Project in 2013, *"One in every three black males born today can expect to go to prison at some point in their life, compared with one in every six Latino males, and one in every 17 white males, if current incarceration trends continue."* The report shows the staggering racial disparities that permeate the American criminal justice system and concludes that *"Racial minorities are more likely than white Americans to be arrested."* The report also explains that *"Once arrested, they are more likely to be convicted; and once convicted; they are more likely to face stiff sentences."* Additionally, *"The disparities don't end with arrests. Because blacks and Hispanics are generally poorer than whites, they are more likely to rely on court appointed public defenders, who tend to work for agencies that are underfunded and understaffed."* Even more alarming is how the criminal justice system's war on drugs directly relates to minority incarceration rates. The report cites *"Racial disparities within the justice system have been exacerbated by the war on drugs. The drug war led the country's population of incarcerated drug offenders to soar from 42,000 in 1980 to nearly half a million in 2007."* From 1999 to 2005, *"African-Americans constituted about 13 percent of drug users, but they made up about 46 percent of those convicted for drug offenses."* [7] Despite the fact that whites and blacks use drugs at similar rates, blacks are jailed on drug charges ten times more often than whites. African-Americans are also three times more likely to be arrested for marijuana than whites, and are sentenced at a much higher rate for the same offences.

In fact, when posed with the question about the equal treatment of people of color in our criminal justice system, many white Americans saw little or no bias in the criminal justice system, yet African-Americans overwhelmingly found the system to be racially biased. This fact alone tells us that Americans still experience two different worlds where their biases and experiences are different based upon their race and ethnicity. Race-based sentencing is the norm in many black and brown communities. African-Americans and other minority groups are prey to the privatized industrial prison system. Not only has the criminal justice system placed a burden on many poverty-stricken African-American communities, but the destruction of families, lack of father figures, and continued disfranchisement of black males in African-American communities has taken its toll on the foundation of the African-American family structure. See Figure 4 below.

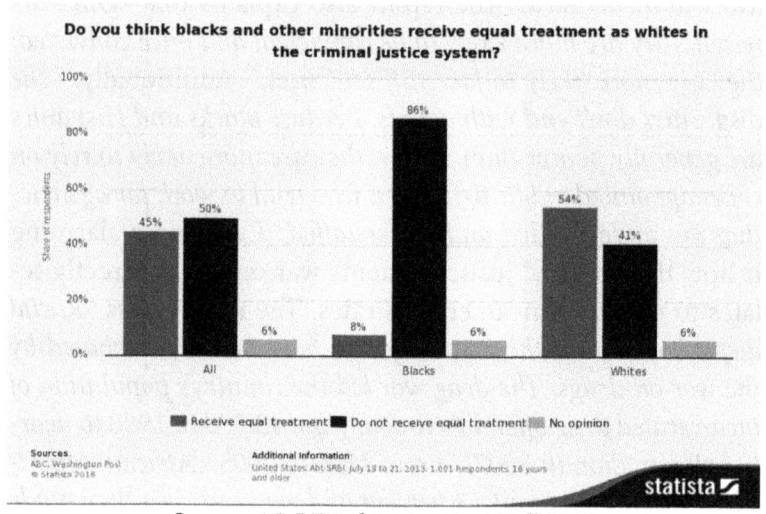

Source: ABC/Washington Post Poll 2013

According to a recent article in the New York Times titled "The Disproportionate Risks of Driving While Black," *In Greensboro, which is 41 percent black, traffic stops help feed the stream of minor charges that draw a mostly African-American crowd of defendants to the county courthouse on weekday mornings. National surveys show that blacks and whites use marijuana at virtually the same rate, but black residents here are charged with the sole offense of possession of minor amounts of marijuana five times as often as white residents are."[8]

Causes for Disparities in our Prison System:

Our society is engulfed in racism and discrimination against African-Americans, and this hatred manifests itself in racial biases in many public policies. Since America's inception, cracks of racism and discrimination against African-Americans have plagued the house of democracy. During the last 300 years, we have made few attempts to fix these cracks, and, as a result, we have struggled with a defective foundation. Thus, here lies the problem of racial hatred in America.

President Bill Clinton's Violent Crime Control and Law Enforcement Act (1994), often termed the *"Crack-Cocaine Law,"* is central to the problem of racial hatred in the American justice system. This act, authored by then-Senator Joe Biden, punished individuals' disproportionally for different types of drug offenses. Once signed into law, this bill created 200,000 new police officer positions, delivered $9.7 billion in new funding for federal prisons, eliminated inmate education programs, expanded the federal death penalty, and codified "three strikes" sentencing mandates at the federal level. President Clinton, himself, said *"I am not going to let anyone who peddles drugs get the idea that the cost of doing business is going down,"* Mr. Clinton said in nullifying a plan by the U.S. Sentencing Commission to make punishments the same for crack cocaine and powdered cocaine."[9]

As a result of this law, people convicted with possession of just five grams of crack cocaine must receive a minimum five-year prison sentence, yet someone must possess five-hundred grams of powdered cocaine to receive the same sentence. According to the US Sentencing Commission, African-Americans account for more than 80 percent of crack cocaine convictions; Whites account for less than 5 percent. As a result of this legislation, African-Americans receive longer sentences for crack cocaine crimes than whites receive for powder-cocaine crimes. The punishment difference of 100 to 1 works as follows: Crimes involving 1 gram of crack get mandatory sentences equal to crimes involving 100 grams of powder. See Figure 5 below, which shows increased incarceration rates since Bill Clinton's signing of the 1994 Crime Bill.

Incarceration rate

Number of people incarcerated per 100,000 population by level of government, 1925-2012

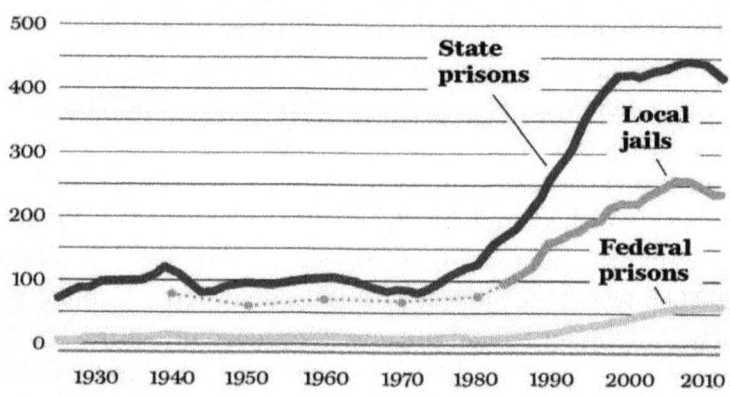

Source: Prison Policy Initiative

Source: Prison Policy Initiative Report 2011

This legislation's effect reaches far in many African-American communities; the law is single handidly responsible for the mass incarceration of African-American males, the building of mass prisons, and the destruction of many African-American families. According Professor Michelle Alexander, "*When Bill left office in 2001, the United States had the highest rate of incarceration in the world. Human Rights Watch reported that in seven states, African-Americans constituted 80 to 90 percent of all drug offenders sent to prison, even though they were no more likely than whites to use or sell illegal drugs. Prison admissions for drug offenses reached a level in 2000 for African-Americans more than 26 times the level in 1983.*" [10]

At a Black Lives Matter rally in spring 2016, a heckler confronted President Bill Clinton about the Violent Crime Control and Law Enforcement Act. Despite defending some parts of the legislation, the former President appeared apologetic for his role in the bill and indicated that the sentencing mandates were too harsh. The former President said "*Yesterday, the President spoke a long time and very well on criminal justice reform…But I want to say a few words about it. Because I signed *a bill that made the problem worse and I want to admit it... The good news is, we had the biggest drop in crime in history... The bad news is we had a lot people who were locked up, who were minor actors, for way too long."* [11]

State of Connecticut: A Case Study:

Connecticut's population is just over 3.5 million residents. The census indicates this population consists of 83 percent whites and just 17 percent Hispanics, African-Americans, Asians, and other ethnic minority groups. Despite this fact, according to statistics from the CT Department of Criminal Justice in 2015, minorities account for about 68 percent of the state's imprisoned population. According to CT Junkie's report, Racial Disparity in Connecticut Prisons, "there was a total of 16,158 people incarcerated in Connecticut, the vast majority of whom are minorities. The report does note that *"Despite the significant decline in the state's prison population across all races, there are still twice as many blacks and Hispanics as whites in Connecticut prisons, even though whites outnumber blacks and Hispanics by an almost 3-to-1 ratio in the state's general population."* [12] For a State that prides itself in racial diversity and commitment towards racial tolerance, Connecticut leads many states in the incarceration minorities for minor crimes and offenses.

Figure 6.

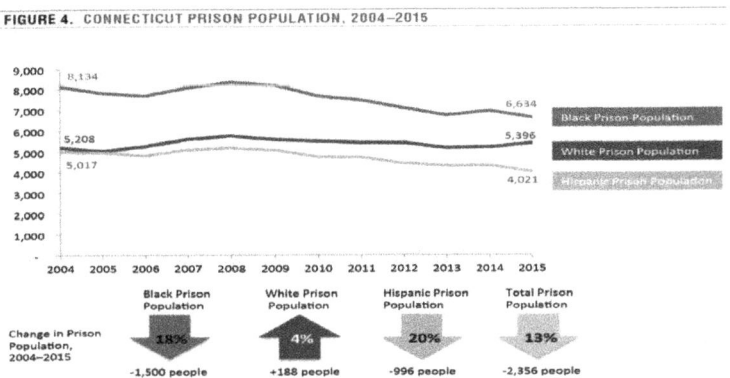

Source: Council of State Government Justice Center 2015 Report.

According to "A Tale of Disproportionate Burden: The special needs of Connecticut's poorer cities," Bridgeport, Hartford, New Haven, and Waterbury report higher crime rates than the state average: *"the crime rate for the state as a whole is 2,981 per 100,000 residents. That figure is 10,114 in Hartford, 7,964 in New Haven, and 6,379 in Waterbury, and 5,435 in Bridgeport."* [13]

According to the report, in 2010 the State of Connecticut implemented additional policies that decriminalized possession of small amounts of marijuana, raised the maximum age of juvenile sentencing within the criminal justice system, instituted a program that created incentives for people in prison to participate in programs that can reduce their risk of reoffending, and adopted a new risk assessment tool to inform parole release decisions. The report states that *"The number of people in prison in Connecticut declined almost 17 percent between January 2008 and January 2015. As of March 2015, there were approximately 16,100 people in Connecticut prisons."*[14] Additionally, the report noted that the number of people in prison *"however, differed across racial groups: whereas the number of whites in the prison population dropped 6 percent during this period, the reduction among blacks and Hispanics, which dropped about 21 percent and 23 percent respectively, was more than three times as steep and served to reduce the long-standing racial disproportion in the state's prisons."* [15]

The data below shows that twice as many African-Americans and Hispanics are in Connecticut prisons than whites, even though whites outnumber blacks and Hispanics by an almost 3-to-1 ratio in the state's general population. Blacks and Hispanics are disproportionally sentenced at a higher rate.

See Figure 7 below.

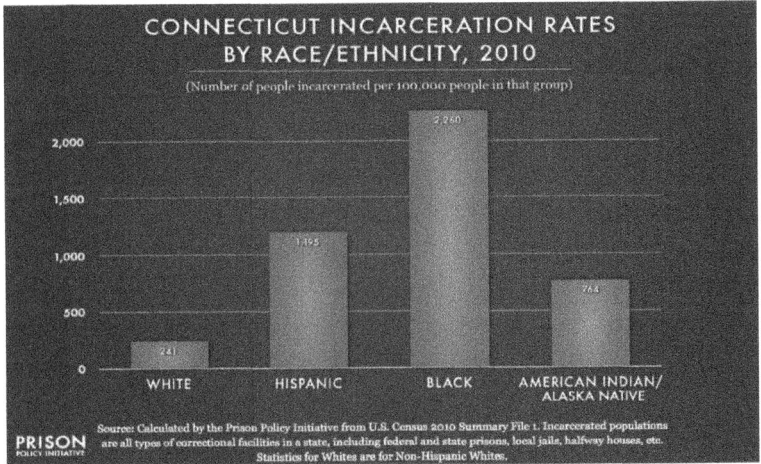

Source: Prison Policy Initiative Report 2013.

Despite making up only about 16% of the State of Connecticut population, minorities account for almost 67% of incarcerated inmates. African-Americans still lead the industrial prison rates when compared to other ethnic groups.

Factors for Incarceration:

No single factor exists that contributes to the higher incarceration rates of minorities in Connecticut, but several elements that play an important role in the prison system. No factor is more important than education and poverty—which I discussed in earlier chapters. The key linkages are: (1) racial segregation and isolation concentrate poverty, (2) economic deprivation, especially unemployment, reduces the pool of marriageable males and increases female headed households, (3) family disruption and concentrated poverty creates the conditions which foster crime, (4) crime destabilizes neighborhoods as those who can move out.[16]

Poverty and Crime:

Crime, poverty, and economic segregation are closely related. Statistics show how crime interacts with economic segregation; as crime increases, we see populations decrease in core inner-city neighborhoods. Whites flee impoverished neighborhoods and move to peripheral areas. As a result, inner cities experience increased crime rates and minority population gain. Termed White Flight, this phenomenon endangers inner cities and leads to the economic abandonment of communities that were once all white. The top five most impoverished cities in Connecticut are Hartford, Waterbury, New Britain, Bridgeport, and New London. Despite continued poverty, these cities, ranked among the poorest in the United States, are located in a state with the nation's highest per capita income. These cities provide important social services for the neediest people in the state, though. As shown below, Hartford, Bridgeport, New Haven, and Waterbury have a disproportionate share of Connecticut's poor. *"Of the total Connecticut population, 1.1 percent receives Temporary Assistance for Needy Families (TANF). Yet, in Hartford, 5.5 percent of the population are TANF recipients, the highest percentage in the state. In Waterbury, 3.8 percent are TANF recipients, while those numbers are 3.6 percent and 2.7 percent for New Haven and Bridgeport, respectively."* [17]

The majority of Connecticut's poor population lives in racially concentrated cities—poor neighborhoods, where many residents face the highest levels of segregation and crime. Experts almost universally agree that poorer communities have higher crime rates; although, debates occur about the roles of unemployment, low income, and economic deprivation in relation to the incarceration of poor people. At a national level, increases in the economic gap directly correlate to crime rates. A report titled "Race, Wealth and Incarceration: Results from the National Longitudinal Survey of Youth" found that impoverished black males were nearly four times more likely to commit crime than impoverished white males; impoverished Hispanics were not far behind blacks. The lack of access to upward economic mobility in many African-American communities is the underlying cause of their frustration and manifests itself in race rebellions, crimes, and riots. America must discuss how to increase upward economic mobility in communities that have been denied their rightful piece of the American economic pie.

Gone from the dialogue is the lack of upward economic mobility and its impact on the crime; gone from the dialogue is the continued economic oppression that plagues inner cities; gone from the dialogue is why many African-Americans and their communities continue to be plagued with economic starvation and poverty. Is there a correlation between economic disparity and crime? The FBI/US Census reports show a significant correlation between the two, as we address the link between poverty and race in America. See Figure 8.

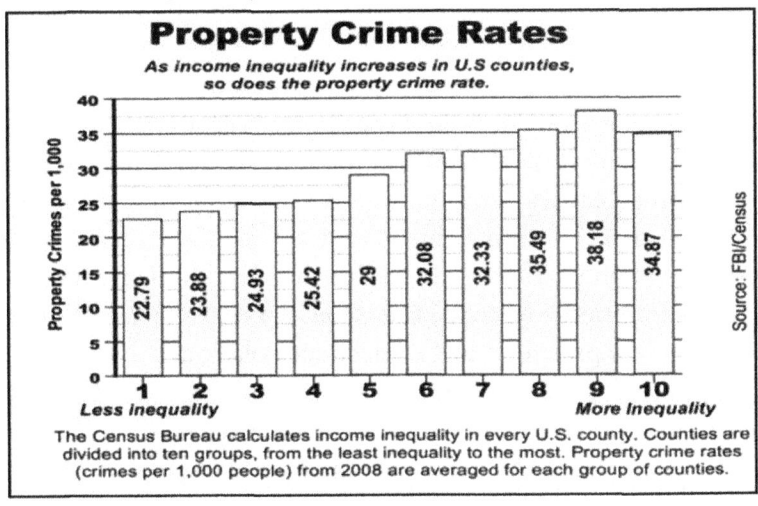

Source: FBI/Census report 2008

The data above show the correlation between economic inequality and increased crime rates as income and opportunities decrease. Many African-American communities that are plagued with systematic racism and a lack of access to upward economic mobility have high crime rates. Often termed the root of all social problems, poverty defines the social ladders of the "haves" and "have nots" in our society. The correlation between legal and systematic racism, exclusion of opportunities that are available to other ethnic groups, and a long history of oppression all play pivotal roles in many black and brown communities. Experts often debate that poverty and crime go hand in hand, that we cannot deal with crime without dealing with the root causes of poverty.

The African-American experience is a 300-year struggle of legalized, systematic racism and oppression in a country that refuses to acknowledge and apologize for its wrongdoing. America refuses to come to terms with this issue and it continues to haunt our society in the 21st century. Thus, this reason is why poverty and crime persist.

Racial Profiling:

According to a recent article in the New York Times titled *"The Disproportionate Risks of Driving While Black,"* traffic stops are many people's most common form of direct interaction with the police; thus, they have a key role in shaping community's perceptions of police. Racial disparities in traffic stops causes certain segments of the population to be exposed to the criminal justice system at higher rates than other segments. These racial differences lead to disparities in the enforcement of laws. This type of racial discrimination is extremely prevalent in Connecticut's black and brown cities-Hartford and Bridgeport-as racial profiling leads to wide disparities in arrests rates. A Connecticut report, *"State of Connecticut Traffic Stop Data Analysis and Findings, 2013-14," found that there were statistically significant racial and ethnic disparities of drivers stopped by police on a statewide level in Connecticut: black and Hispanic drivers were both stopped at a much higher rate and searched at a much higher rate than white drivers. However, white drivers are much more likely than drivers of color to be found to possess contraband in their vehicles as a result of a search."* [18] This finding suggests that, despite Connecticut's racial profiling laws, mistrust lingers between law enforcement officials and Connecticut's minority population.

According to Central Connecticut State University's Institute for Municipal and Regional Policy, "*Black drivers were nearly twice as likely as white drivers to be stopped by police in Connecticut, and blacks stopped were twice as likely as whites to have their vehicles searched, according to a compilation of 360,000 traffic stops from Oct. 1, 2013, through May 31, 2014.*"[19] The report also indicated that "*The Hartford suburb of Farmington, for example, has a black population of just 1.62 percent, while 7.88 percent of all motorists stopped were black. That would indicate blacks were nearly five times more likely to be stopped – until the data is adjusted to reflect that Farmington's daytime population is larger and more diverse than its resident population.*"[20] Given these statistics, we can conclude that racial profiling of minorities is rampant across Connecticut's suburbs.

According to Scott X. Esdaile, President of the State's NAACP, "*We have a serious problem in the state of Connecticut, and now we have the facts to validate it...Now it's imperative for us to roll up our sleeves and do the right thing to eradicate it.*"[21] An analysis of more than 586,000 traffic stops between October 2014 and September 2015 identified five police departments and one state police troop where there was "*a statistically significant racial or ethnic disparity [in traffic stops] that may indicate the presence of racial and ethnic bias.*"[22] Consequently, aspects of black life, including various forms of exploitation and social disenfranchisement, tend to go unaddressed in communities comprised mostly of whites. On the other hand, media tends to demonize young black males by sensationalizing crimes-such as homicide, rape, robbery, and drug dealing-that affect the inner city; research shows, though, that only a small percentage of black males are responsible for such crimes.

According to Kelly Welch, "*Racial stereotyping of criminals has been an enduring and unfortunate feature, the stereotyping of Blacks as criminals is so pervasive throughout society that 'criminal predator' is used as a euphemism for 'young Black male'. This common stereotype has erroneously served as a subtle rationale for the unofficial policy and practice of racial profiling by criminal justice practitioner of American culture." [23] Despite Connecticut's legislature passing laws which emphatically prohibit racial-profiling and discrimination, people of color continued to file complaints about their encounters with a predominantly white police force.

Education:
The relationship between education and incarceration rates remains the pivotal reason behind the high incarceration of many young African-American and Hispanic men. There is a defining link between a poor education, lack of education, and incarceration of individuals. Reports suggest that high school dropouts are 3.5 times more likely to be arrested than high school graduates. At a national level, 68 percent of all males in prison do not have a high school diploma; many inmates possess the literacy rate of an average eight grader. According to Marc H. Morial, President of the National Urban League, *"The dropout rate is driving the nation's increasing prison population, and it's a drag on America's economic competitiveness."* [24]

A 2013 report from the Alliance for Excellent Education titled "Saving Futures, Saving Dollars: The Impact of Education on Crime Reduction and Earnings" examines the connection between low levels of educational attainment and high rates of arrests and incarceration. The reported indicated that *"There is an indirect correlation between educational attainment and arrest and incarceration rates, particularly among males, the report finds. According to the most recent data from the U.S. Bureau of Justice, 56 percent of federal inmates, 67 percent of inmates in state prisons, and 69 percent of inmates in local jails did not complete high school. Additionally, the number of incar-*

cerated individuals without a high school diploma is increasing over time. 'Dropping out of school does not automatically result in a life of crime, but high school dropouts are far more likely than high school graduates to be arrested or incarcerated." [25] Among African-Americans who have matured during the era of mass incarceration, one in four has had a parent incarcerated at some point during their childhood. For black men in their 20's and 30's without high school diplomas, the incarceration rate is so high-nearly 40 percent nationwide-that they're more likely to be behind bars than to have a job.

Bob Wise, president of the Alliance for Excellent Education, stated *"The nation needs to focus dollars and efforts on reforming school climates to keep students engaged in ways that will lead them toward college and a career and away from crime and prison,"* [26] He further elaborated that *"The school-to-prison pipeline starts and ends with schools."* [27] According to a DOJ report (2003), over 90 percent of the prison population is male, almost half is black, and the data available at this point indicate that 40 percent have not completed high school. Prison populations' rapid growth and the particularly high incarceration rate for uneducated black males have focused scholarly attention on several different aspects of the educational characteristics of prisoners. [28] See Figure 9 below.

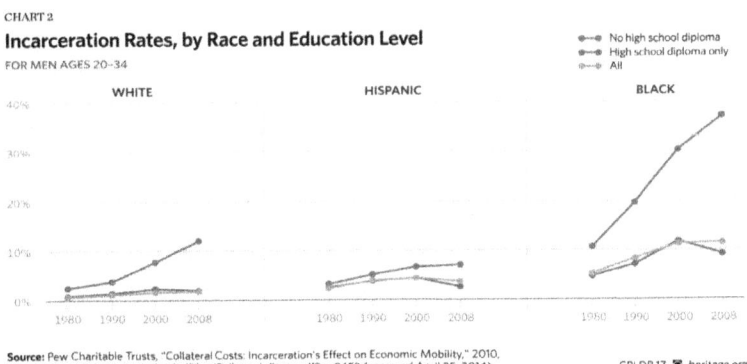

Source: Pew Charitable Trust 2010 Report.

The data above show the correlation of education inequality and the increased crime rates. As levels of education increase, incarceration rates decrease among people of color. The assumption that higher levels of educational attainment-college degrees, high school diplomas, et cetera-will help reduce crime is philosophical debate. Whether direct or indirect, a correlation exists between the lack of educational attainment, arrest, and incarceration rates among people of color. According to the most recent data from the U.S. Bureau of Justice 2013, 56 percent of federal inmates, 67 percent of inmates in state prisons, and 69 percent of inmates in local jails did not complete high school. Additionally, the number of incarcerated individuals without a high school diploma is increasing. According to Bob Wise, president of the Alliance for Excellent Education, *"Dropping out of school does not automatically result in a life of crime, but high school dropouts are far more likely than high school graduates to be arrested or incarcerated."* [29]

The Role of Mass Media:

The love-hate relationship with Mass Media plays a crucial role in the way white Americans perceive African-Americans, as a result of the overwhelming media focus on *"crime, drug use, gang violence, welfare, prison incarceration rates, school dropout rates, music and other forms of anti-social behavior among African-Americans, the media have fostered a distorted and pernicious public perception of African-Americans."* [30] The media has not studied either important events in the African-American community today or this community's immense contributions to the American society. Issues such as urbanization, education, poverty, and other elements have a significant bearing on positions of the black community. A good example of media bias is the media portrayal of the Los Angeles riots in 1992. According to former Harvard

University's African-American Studies Professor Cornel West, *"what we witnessed in Los Angeles was the consequence of a lethal linkage of economic decline, cultural decay, and political lethargy in American life. Race was the visible catalyst, not the underlying cause, as media portrayed it to be."* [31]

This individual event's portrayal encouraged the perception that the black community was solely responsible for the riots and disturbances. According to reports of those arrested, *"only 36 percent were black and of those arrested, more than a third had full-time jobs and most had no political affiliation."* [32] Roughly 60 percent of the rioters and looters consisted of Hispanics and whites, yet the media did not report this underlying fact. The media portrayal of this event, along with other race riots, inflicts scorn on black awareness. The 1980 race riots in Miami were similar to the Los Angeles riots. Here, the media also refused to search for the underlying cause behind the protest, choosing instead only to depict African-American males engaged in violence and destruction. The underlying factors behind these problems were never researched or explained in media coverage. The media has taken a step further in Hollywood. Here, the portrayal of young African-American males (involved in gangs and other deviant acts of violence) is a multimillion-dollar industry. American society now accepts the stereotypes that the film media ascribes to the black community. Films such as *Boyz in the Hood* and *Menace II Society* are multimillion-dollar success stories with criminal portrayals of young blacks.

Over time, this portrayal fosters false beliefs in white America regarding the way they perceive blacks. Given the situation in America, where the major news media has predominantly white reporters and serves a mainly white audience, it follows that the "public" that dictates newsworthy events is a white public. The day-to-day tensions of black existence and exploitation are not primary concerns of the white public. Only the symptoms of these conditions, such as freedom rides and social disturbances, impinge upon whites. Hence, the white press only reports such "events," not their social causes.

One of the main reasons for the inadequate coverage of the racial stereotypes' underlying causes in the U.S. is that the black condition itself is not a matter of interest for the white majority. Their interest in black America focuses upon situations where their imagined fears become real problems. Events like boycotts, pickets, civil rights demonstrations, and racial violence mark the point at which black activity impinges on white concerns. The white-oriented media seeks to satisfy the needs of their white audience and reflects this pattern of attention to these selected events. Research discloses that most *"serious crimes (homicide, rape, robbery, and assault) in inner cities are committed by a very small proportion of African-American youth, some 8 percent by estimates."* [33] Yet the tendency to characterize all African-American males as criminals prevails in our society. As a result of these stereotypes, law officers now commonly stop young black males and harass them.

According to a report released by the Wall Street Journal in 2011, the role of media racial bias continues well into the 21st century. The Journal suggests that black and Hispanic New Yorkers are disproportionately targeted for "stop and frisk" pat-downs. The report, also, finds that of the 684,330 "stops" initiated by NYPD officers from January 2010 through 2011, almost 87 percent were of blacks and Hispanics, despite the fact that those groups comprise less than half of the City's population. In contrast, only 13 percent of stops were of white New Yorkers, a group that comprises 43 percent of the City's population.[34]

Figure 10 below.

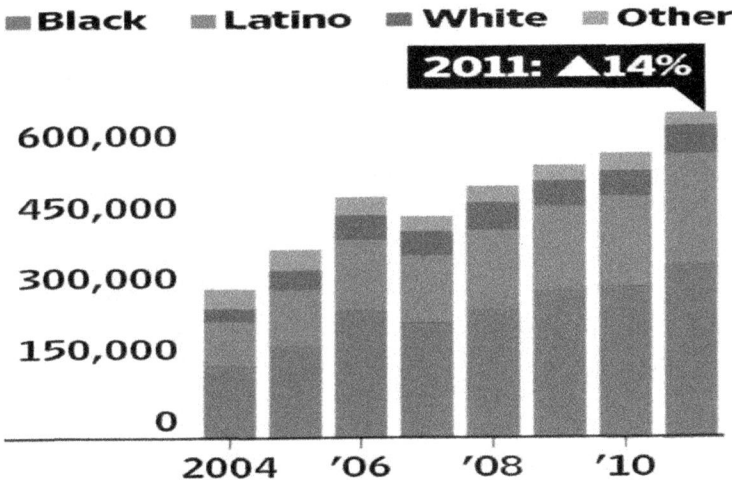

Source: The Wall Street Journal. February 2012

So while the media continues focusing on criminal and deviant behavior, no one is praising the college success rates of young blacks. Negative stereotypes continue to affect the black community, as well as their prospects for employment and advancement. These stereotypes contribute to high crimes within the African-American community.

Conclusion:

Whatever the arguments are, a direct connection between race, racism, and our criminal justice system exists. The underlying issue remains that races plays an important part in all public policy implementation. Race defines who we are as Americans and often takes away the best of what we can become as a society.

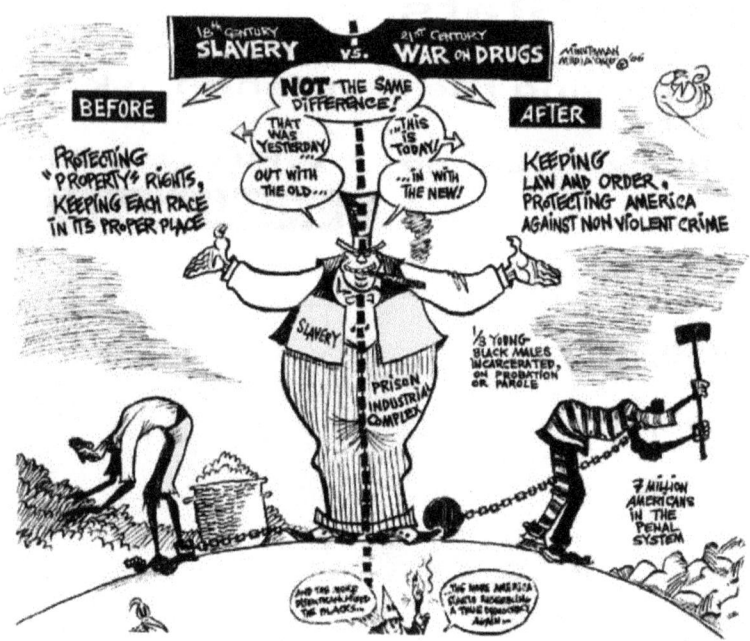

Source: http://www.learnliberty.org/videos/racial-inequality-in-the-criminal-justice-system/

References:
1. http://newjimcrow.com/about/excerpt-from-the-introduction
2. http://www.nccdglobal.org/sites/default/files/publication_pdf/created-equal.pdf
3. http://www.huffingtonpost.com/antonio-moore/black-mass-incarceration-statistics_b_6682564.html
4. http://www.sentencingproject.org/wp-content/uploads/2016/01/Reducing-Racial-Disparity-in-the-Criminal-Justice-System-A-Manual-for-Practitioners-and-Policymakers.pdf
5. The Center for American Progress: A Look at the Racial Disparities Inherent in Our Nation's Criminal-Justice System. March 2012
6. Michael Sclafani's Civil Rights in Present Day America
7. Sentencing Project report's Regarding Racial Disparities in the United States Criminal Justice System 2013
8. http://www.nytimes.com/2015/10/25/us/racial-disparity-traffic-stops-driving-black.html?_r=0
9. http://articles.baltimoresun.com/1995-10-31/news/1995304052_1_crack-cocaine-powder-cocaine-cocaine-crimes
10. ://www.theroot.com/articles/politics/2016/02/the_clinton_legacy_decimated_black_america_so_why_are_we_still_voting_for/2/
11. http://www.cnn.com/2015/07/15/politics/bill-clinton-1994-crime-bill/
12. http://hartfordinfo.org/issues/wsd/taxes/ccm-poorer-cities.pdf
13. http://hartfordinfo.org/issues/wsd/taxes/ccm-poorer-cities.pdf
14. Ibid
15. Ibid
16. http://www.ssc.wisc.edu/~oliver/RACIAL/Reports/nsfAug01narrative.pdf

17. http://hartfordinfo.org/issues/wsd/taxes/ccm-poorer-cities.pdf
18. http://www.nytimes.com/2015/10/25/us/racial-disparity-traffic-stops-driving-black.html?_r=0
19. Central Connecticut State University's Institute for Municipal and Regional Policy Report on Racial Profiling 2014
20. Ibid
21. http://www.courant.com/data-desk/hc-are-people-of-color-more-likely-to-get-pulled-over-in-certain-connecticut-towns-20140918-htmlstory.html
22. http://www.courant.com/opinion/editorials/
23. Kelly Welch: Black Criminal Stereotypes and Racial Profiling
24. http://www.nytimes.com/2009/10/09/education/09dropout.html
25. http://all4ed.org/press/crime-rates-linked-to-educational-attainment-new-alliance-report-finds/
26. http://all4ed.org/press/crime-rates-linked-to-educational-attainment-new-alliance-report-finds/
27. Ibid
28. Harlow, Caroline. 2003. "Education and Correctional Populations." U.S. Department of Justice, Bureau of Justice Statistics Special Report. January 2003.
29. http://all4ed.org/press/crime-rates-linked-to-educational-attainment-new-alliance-report-finds/
30. Taylor, R. (1995, March 19). The harm brought by racial stereotype. Hartford Courant , p. D4.
31. West, C. (1993). Race matters. Cambridge, MA: Blackwell Press 1993.
32. Ibid
33. Taylor, R. (1995, March 19). The harm brought by racial stereotype. Hartford Courant , p. D4.
34. http://www.wsj.com/articles/SB10001424052970204795304577221770752633612

Chapter 7
Healthcare Disparities

> *"Many black people in the United States get their primary healthcare in a separate and apparently inferior system. When black patients go to the doctor, they're more likely to be treated by a doctor who can't harness the full capabilities of the healthcare system."* [1]
> -Dr. Peter B. Bach, Epidemiologist at Memorial Sloan-Kettering Cancer Center in New York.

Universal healthcare has long been a goal of our democratic society; how we achieve and implement this goal has been impeded by challenges and obstacles from corporate healthcare companies. The Unites States with its prosperity and vast wealth, a healthcare system that has often been termed the Rolls Royce of the developed world. Yet, at the same time there is an association between healthcare outcomes and treatment that are specifically tied to race, ethnicity, and socioeconomic status. This has left an undeniable disparity in ways certain ethnic and racial group receive their medical treatment in the USA. According to a report by the CDC, "In recent decades, the United States has made substantial progress in improving our residents' health and reducing dis-

parities, but ongoing economic, racial/ethnic other social disparities in health still exist." [2] Yet subsequent reports suggest that our medical system has been more segregated than previously thought; that in fact, there is a dual system of healthcare for blacks and whites. We have created an apartheid healthcare system that caters to one racial ethnic group and discriminate against others.

According the American Medical Association (AMA), physicians who treat many black patients were less likely to be board-certified and more likely to struggle to provide high-quality care than physicians who treat white patients. Dr. Peter B. Bach, an epidemiologist at Memorial Sloan-Kettering Cancer Center in New York who was the lead author of the study in the New England Journal of Medicine, concluded that *"many black people in the United States get their primary healthcare in a separate and apparently inferior system."* He also stated 'When black patients go to the doctor, they're more likely to be treated by a doctor who can't harness the full capabilities of the healthcare system."* [3]

The idea that a healthcare system that provides for one ethnic group at the expense of another remains a message lost in the struggle for equality in America and the guarantee for Civil Rights for all. According to the American Medical Association report in 2013 *"Recent studies have shown that despite the steady improvements in the overall health of the United States, racial and ethnic minorities experience a lower quality of health services and are less likely to receive routine medical procedures and have higher rates of morbidity and mortality than non-minorities."* [4] The way we administer and provide healthcare has always been divided along racial and socio economic lines. African-Americans and Hispanics who fall into these groups tend to be more at risk to the disparities, due to their lack of access to same caliber of services available to their white counterparts. These disparities may take shape in all forms in the medical profession diseases such as heart disease, diabetes, cancer, HIV and other illness continue to plague communities that do not have access to quality medical education and treatment. The key to this research is why does it exist and what are the solutions?

In Justin Dimick's Healthcare Racial Disparities, he cites two main reasons why we continue to see disparities between whites and ethnic minorities groups. His first theory addresses the cultural competence of minority groups in America, where is claims *"many of the gaps in care are due to poor communication between providers and patients. Given the long history of discrimination against black Americans, the cultural competency theory argues that low trust on the part of patients, combined with the ineffective communication and lack of cultural sensitivity, leads to black patients receiving worse care with resultant poor outcomes."* [5] His second theory on why disparities exist in many ethnic communities refers to *"the site of care really matters, that disparities are driven by the fact that black patients are more likely to receive care at poor quality hospitals, this he claims shows that care for black patients is highly concentrated among a small number of hospitals and these places generally provide a lower quality of care for all their patients."* [6] Whatever the arguments are, this apartheid healthcare system continues even in the midst of the post racial America in which we all believe that equality and access to resources are guaranteed to all despite our color and socio-economic status.

Historical Background:

As we reflect on Martin Luther King's day 2017, it is a heart wrenching realization that we celebrate his commitment to justice for all once a year, but as educators, researchers, healthcare providers and as Americans we fail to promote his dream daily. Today our nation has a 34% non-white race and is trending towards a minority majority population by 2050. This multicultural population and our beliefs regarding healthcare must be considered in the care of the population we serve. Attitudes towards how we serve the new America remain divisive. Not until the signing of the Healthcare Research and Quality Act of 1999, did the United State (US) Congress mandate the Agency for Healthcare Research and Quality (AHRQ) to annually report on healthcare quality and disparities in the US. To meet the requirements of the Healthcare Research and Quality Act of 1999, the AHRQ annually produces two reports: The National Healthcare Quality Report (NHQR) and the National Healthcare Disparities Report (NHDR). These reports include performance measures to evaluate the US's progress towards providing universal high quality healthcare for all. The NHQR's goal is to describe quality of healthcare in the US, while the goal of the NHDR is to report racial, ethical and socioeconomic disparities in healthcare (Siegel, Moy, Burstin, 2004).

In 2003, the first National Healthcare Quality Report and the National Healthcare Disparities Report were published by the AHRQ reporting progress results and illuminating opportunities for reducing healthcare disparities. These reports can and should be used to improve quality of care provided to all Americans to narrow the gap in racial, ethnic and socioeconomic disparities across the nation. Unfortunately, improvement in quality healthcare among minority races and narrowing the gap in delivery of quality of healthcare is not being done. The NHQR shows that disparities in high quality healthcare and access to healthcare continue to exist despite attempts to bridge the gap. (Siegel, Moy, Burstin, 2004).

The first sub-domain of Quality of Healthcare is effectiveness; this subdomain pertains to cancer, chronic kidney disease, diabetes, heart disease, HIV/AID, mental health and respiratory disease. Other subdomains for Quality of Healthcare are patient safety, timeliness of treatment and patient-centeredness. The domain of Access to Healthcare is comprised of 5 subdomains: entry into the healthcare system, structural barriers within the healthcare system patient's perceptions of provider's ability to address patient needs, healthcare utilization and healthcare cost. The 2010 NHDR report showed that African-Americans and American Indians/Alaska Natives received worse care than their White counterparts in 40 percent of quality of care measures. Hispanics received worse care than non-Hispanic Whites in 60 percent of the quality of care measures. Asian-Americans received worse care than Whites for 20% of the measures.

Disparities in access to healthcare realistically contribute to the imbalance in quality of healthcare. This indicates that access to healthcare should have been addressed first. Related to access to care, African-Americans had 33 percent worse access to care of core measures than Whites. Hispanics had 83 percent worse access to care for core measures than non-Hispanic Whites. The largest identifiable racial and ethnic healthcare disparities show little evidence of narrowing or improving. The concluding report suggests that the nation needs to take action to accelerate progress towards providing universal high quality healthcare for all minorities.

See Figure 1.

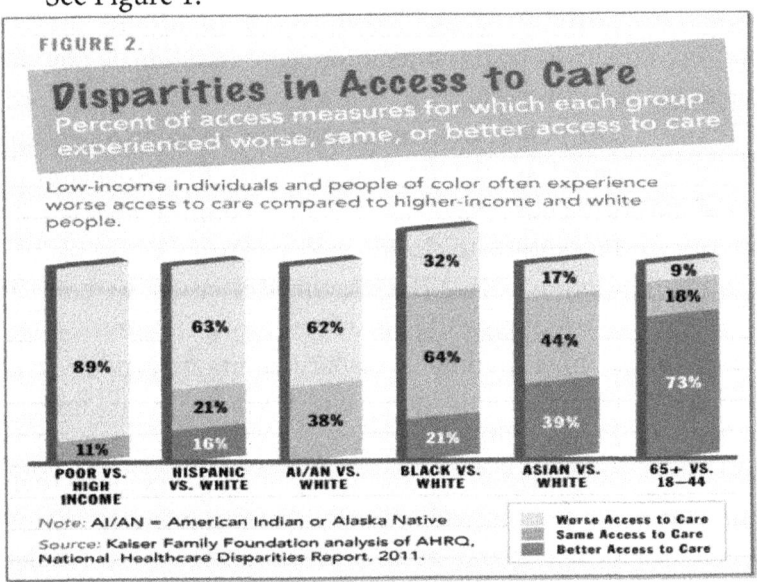

Source: KCMU/Urban Institute Report 2012.

The data above shows the continued disparity with regard to access the care, many communities with lower incomes families and those that have a higher percentage of minorities are plagued with shortages of quality health service providers.

Quality of Healthcare:

In 2004, African-Americans, Hispanic Americans and American Indians combined made up more than 25 percent of the U.S. population but only 9 percent of the nation's nurses, 6 percent of its physicians and 5 percent of dentists. Similar disparities appeared in the faculties of health professional schools. For example, minorities made up less than 10 percent of baccalaureate nursing faculties, 8.6 percent of dental school faculties and only 4.2 percent of medical school faculties. (Adler N, Reaching for a Healthier Life: Facts on Socioeconomic Status and Health in the United States, the *John D. and Catherine T. MacArthur Foundation Research Network on Socioeconomic Status and Health*) One of the key goals of the Affordable Care Act (ACA) is to reduce the number of uninsured through the expansion of Medicaid the creation of health insurance exchange marketplaces with advance premium tax credits to help moderate-income individuals pay for their medical coverage.

Given that people of color are at disproportionate risk of being uninsured and having low incomes, the expansion of ACA coverage could particularly benefit communities of color and advance efforts to eliminate disparities. (Kaiser Family Foundation Report 2013) Despite this legislation, we continue to see persistent growing dipartites among the ethnic races in America. These modifiable disparities among gender, race, ethnicity, socioeconomic status and disability status impact both their chronic illness and acute health outcomes. African-Americans have a life expectancy of 3.8 years lower than the white population, with African-American males having the lowest life expectancy at 4.7 years lowers than white males (Kochanek, Arias, Anderson, 2013). Although life expectancy for the African-American population has increased by 17% since 1970, there are certain disparities in healthcare quality that are worsening over time (AHRQ, 2014; Kochanek, Arias, Anderson, 2013). See Figure 2.

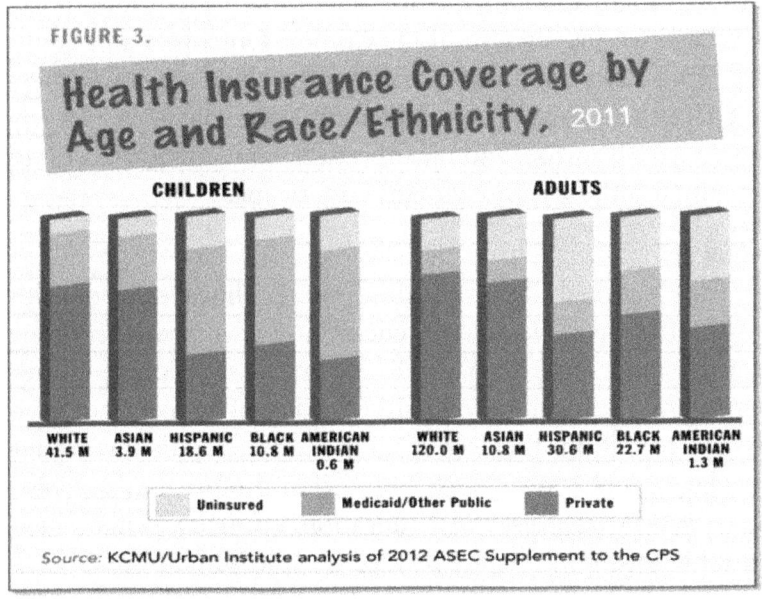

Source: KCMU/Urban Institute Report 2012.

According to the CDC, African-American infants are twice more likely to die before their first birthday than Caucasian infants as compared to other races. During childbirth, African-American mothers are three times more likely to die than Caucasian mothers due to lack of preventative care and access to quality health services (CDC, 2011). Statistics show that obesity, coronary heart disease, diabetes and HIV also have significant differences in comparison of rates by race and gender. African-Americans have much higher coronary heart disease death rates than other races. (CDC, 2011) Other reports show that worsening disparities are found with patients with breast cancer diagnosed at advanced stage in ages 40 and over, maternal deaths per 100,000 live births and adults age 40 and over with diagnosed diabetes. (AHRQ, 2014).

According to a CBS report *"It is widely accepted that African-Americans have higher mortality and worse cardiovascular outcomes in the general population. A large part of this is attributable to socioeconomic deprivation, which includes, among others, lack of obtaining needed healthcare."* [7] study author Dr. Csaba Kovesdy, director of the Clinical Outcomes and Clinical Trials Program in Nephrology at the University of Tennessee Health Science Center. These disparities have been largely attributed to socioeconomic differences and unequal access to quality healthcare among many Americans.

Cancer:

The National Cancer Institute (NCI) defines "cancer health disparities" as adverse differences in cancer incidence (new cases), cancer prevalence (all existing cases), cancer death (mortality), cancer survivorship burden of cancer or related health conditions that exist among specific population groups in the United States. These population groups may be characterized by age, disability, education, ethnicity, gender, geographic location, income or race. People who are poor, lack health insurance and are medically underserved (have limited or no access to effective healthcare)—regardless of ethnic and racial background—often bear a greater burden of disease than the general population. (NCI 2014 report)

According to the America Cancer Society Cancer Action Network, "the underlying causes of cancer disparities are interrelated and complex. Causes of cancer disparities can be linked to social, behavioral economic factors such as persistent inequalities in access to care, language barriers, unhealthy environments racial discrimination. The consequences of such fundamental causes of disparities are that diseases like cancer are more often diagnosed at later stages when the severity is likely to be greater and options for treatment, as well as the odds of survival, are decreased." (ACSCAN, 2009 Report) They further concluded that racial and ethnic minorities and persons of lower socioeconomic status are more likely to engage in high risk health behaviors and less likely to receive timely cancer screenings. African-American women are 40 percent more likely to die of breast cancer than white women. The Center for Disease Control and Prevention reports multiple factors contribute to these statistics, including more aggressive cancers and fewer social and economic resources. (CDC, 2012) Studies have also shown that race or ethnicity predict the likelihood of an individual's or a group's access to education, certain occupations, health insurance living conditions including conditions where exposure to environmental toxins most common all of which are associated with the risk of developing and surviving cancer.

In 2010, African-American and white women reported equal breast cancer screening, however African America women were found to have breast cancer that spread beyond the breast more frequently than white women. African-American women's post mammogram follow-up was later treatment was started later compared to white women. Only 69 percent of African-American women started treatment within 30 days, compared to 83 percent of white women (CDC, 2012 report). This report shows the continued disproportion with regard to treatment of the disease among the races, which correlates among the vast differences in the cancer death rate among women. See Figure 3 below.

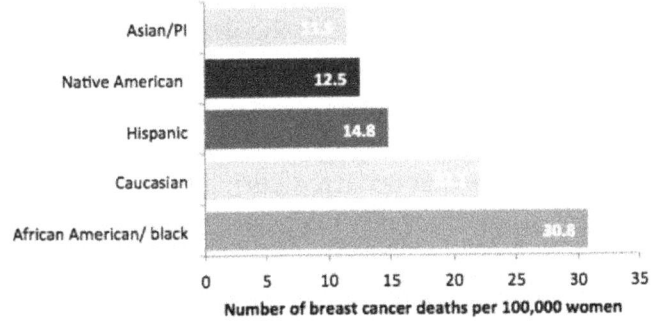

Source. Susan G. Komen Report 2006-2010

The America Cancer Society Cancer Action Network concluded that racial and ethnic minorities, persons of lower socioeconomic status the uninsured are more likely to be diagnosed with some cancers often at later stages when the severity is likely to be greater and the odds of survival are decreased. Access to adequate healthcare coverage can make a difference in the fight against cancer. Lack of medical coverage, barriers to early detection and screening unequal access to improvements in cancer treatment may contribute to observed differences in survival between African-American/Black and White women.

According to the CDC, adopting a healthy lifestyle and receiving recommended health screenings are first steps. Unfortunately, not all communities have the same access to resources and healthcare services necessary for a healthy lifestyle and early detection of diseases like heart disease, cancer diabetes. Poor access to care, a lack of health insurance the fear of seeking medical care because of immigration status is among the biggest barriers. There is also a complex mixture of individual and societal factors that is behind the health disparities affecting people of color and, experts say, it is the conditions on the following pages that are among those that have a significant impact on them. (CDC Report on Minority Communities 2011)

Infant Mortality:

Infant mortality is defined as the death of a child within the first year of life the measure of the extent of infant mortality in a population is the infant mortality rate (IMR). IMR is calculated as the number of infant deaths in a period of time per 1,000 live births that occurred during the same time period. In recent infant mortality rates have declined dramatically in the United States. However, the gap between black and white mortality rates continues to increase projections indicate that this trend will continue to grow. Studies have shown that despite improvements in infant mortality rates over time, disparities by race and ethnicity still persist in many black and brown communities.

The infant mortality rate for African-American women was 2.4 times higher than white women and persistent racial or ethnical disparities continue to exist in infant mortality and low birth weight. (AHRQ, 2014) In 2007, infant mortality rates for black women were primarily due to higher rates of preterm birth and preterm-related causes of death. Fifty-five percent of the black-white infant mortality gap is due to preterm related causes (MacDorman & Mathews, 2011). As studies show, racial health disparity is worsening for African-Americans compared to whites is maternal deaths per 100,000 live births, the maternal mortality rate among Black women was approximately 2.7 times the rate for non-Hispanic White women. (Xu, Kochanek, Murphy, & Tejada-Vera, 2010) See Figure 4 below.

Figure 4. Infant Mortality Rates among the Ethnic Races. 2013

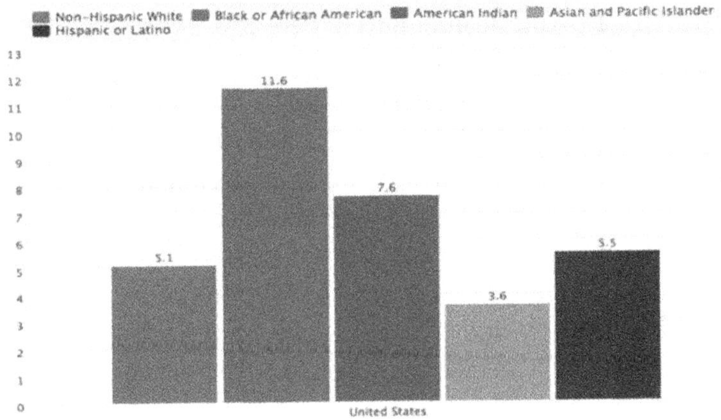

Source: Annie Casey Foundation Report on Infant Mortality 2013.

The above report concluded that, although still higher than most other developed countries, the U.S. infant mortality rate has declined by 34% since 1990. Developments in maternal health and advancements in medical technology partially explain the trend. Despite improvements, racial disparities persist, with African-American (11.6 per 1,000 live births) and American Indian (7.6 per 1,000 live births) infants experiencing higher mortality rates when compared to their white counterparts. (ACF Infant Mortality report 2013)

The American Academy of Pediatrics (AAP) recommends 7 preventative healthcare visits for all children before 12 months of age, 3 between 12-30 months of age then once yearly. Research shows that African-American children have lower rates of well-child visits compared with white children; while Hispanic children had lower rates than White, Black other non-Hispanic children (AHRQ, 2014). Preventative measures include immunizations are important to reduce mortality, a target for Healthy People 2020 is 80 percent of children in the US to be up-to data on vaccines in the age range of 19-35 months according to the USDHHS (United States Department of Health and Human Services [HHS], Healthy People 2020, 2011). Despite this goal, reports still show that from 2007 to 2011, African-American children were less likely than white children to receive all recommended vaccinations that are required by the USDHHS. (AHRQ, 2014)

Healthcare disparities come at a high price, poorly managed care, missed diagnoses, unequal treatment in many minorities serve communities and the access to high quality care all perpetuate a national disaster that will soon affect all Americans. Despite advancements in treatment and services to newborns, there still remains a gap among the socio-economic class and the racial ethnic groups with regard to the survival rates of newborns.

Heart Disease:

The department of Health and Human Services (HHS) defines a racial or ethnic health disparity as *"a particular type of health difference that is closely linked with social, economic /or environmental disadvantage. Health disparities adversely affect groups of people who have systematically experienced greater obstacles to health based on their racial or ethnic group."* [8] The number one cause of death among Americans can be attributed to heart disease and obesity, despite the decline of heart disease death rates over the last decade, the racial gap among peoples of color continue to persist. According to the AMA 2013 report, *"The origins of disparities in CVD are numerous and wide-ranging, including variations in the type, awareness and presentation of symptoms and the response to them."* These disparities (gender, SES, ethnicity/race) have largely evolved from inequalities in society. Similarly, disparities in CVD, interventions and outcomes will also vary depending on the minority or disadvantaged group and their socio-economic status.

A person's race or ethnicity should not put them more at risk for having heart disease or stroke, but unfortunately, it is one factor that affects a person's likeliness of suffering a heart attack or stroke and chances of survival if they do. Cardiovascular disease (CVD), including heart disease and stroke, remains the No. 1 killer of Americans and exacts a disproportionate toll on many racial and ethnic groups that have higher rates of CVD and its risk factors. For example, CVD accounts for about one-third of the disparity in potential life-years lost between blacks and whites. The background of these disparities can be a number of reasons not more important than the access to quality healthcare and inequalities that persist in many poor socio-economic communities. According to Jennifer Lewey & Niteesh K. Choudhry in an article in the Public Health Policy, *"Differences in the quality of healthcare delivered to minority versus non-minority populations are attributed to several complex causes, including differences in clinical presentation, patient preference, access to care, health insurance options social environment. Furthermore, discrimination and the biases of some providers and health systems contribute to the differential treatment of certain groups."* [9]

From an Editorial published in the International Journal of Cardiology titled "Gender, socioeconomic and ethnic/racial disparities in cardiovascular disease: A time for change," the authors cite the following conclusions *"People who are socioeconomically disadvantaged experience higher rates of CVD burden and mortality. Originally, CVD and its risk factors were more common in upper socioeconomic groups in the developed world, but over the past 50 years this pattern has reversed and the differential widened. The inverse association between SES and CVD risk in high-income countries is the result of compounding behavioral and psychosocial risk factors. Not only are low SES groups more exposed to cardiovascular risks such as smoking, alcohol consumption, physical inactivity and poor diet, disadvantaged socioeconomic conditions are also known to disproportionately increase this risk across the life course. In addition to poor health behaviors, people in low SES groups have less access to medical care and social support, greater co-morbidity and job stress poorer health."* [10] The solutions to these continuing disparities are not limited to any one factor but must be a number of policies and procedures that in one way or another assist in bridging the nation's great divide.

Coalitions between communities, healthcare community-based organizations, state and local governments' education healthcare policies, access to healthcare programs educating the public on all sectors of healthcare are essential. Center to the debate is also individual responsibility, according to Horner RD, Salazar W, Geiger HJ, l. "Changing healthcare professionals' behaviors to eliminate disparities in healthcare: *"Individual responsibility and behavior change are important but must be supplemented with widespread policy and systems changes in the healthcare setting. We must engage the active participation and leadership of federal agencies, state and local governments, policy makers, healthcare provider's health professional organizations in these endeavors. Several working models that have successfully reduced health disparities in managed care and oth-*

er settings have been published and are being used by public, private, commercial Medicaid managed-care organizations." [11] They argue that in order to have a successful implementation of policies we must put in place the following common goals: providing care, education, rebuilding an efficient healthcare system, emphasis on prevention, disease tracking and last but by no means least government healthcare programs that serve all.

Access to Healthcare:

It can easily be argued that disparities in quality of healthcare will not improve until disparities in access to healthcare improve. These disparities, related to race and ethnicity, can be contributed to a multitude of social and physical factors including access to care and the view of the healthcare system. Improvement in health disparities related to ethnicity will not be realized until there is an improvement in lifestyle choices, positive healthcare interventions including appropriate screening, early diagnosis, patient education, timely treatment and routine follow up of chronic conditions.

Reports have always confirmed what healthcare scholars have been saying for decades, which is, that our healthcare system is broken and racially biased. Gail C. Christopher, the former Vice President of the Joint Center for Political and Economic Studies Office of Health, Women and Families and current vice president for Health at the WK Kellogg Foundation, wrote: "National surveys have consistently confirmed the simple and primary reason why people are uninsured—they cannot afford to purchase health insurance if their employers don't offer and pay for health insurance. Compared to white Americans, studies show that African Americans are less likely to work in jobs that make health insurance available, they are less likely to be offered health insurance they are less likely to take it when offered. Just 53% of African Americans get insurance through work as compared to 72% of white Americans.... "*African Americans constitute 12% of the overall population but 16% of the uninsured. 53% of African Americans earn less than 200% FPL [Federal Poverty Level] as compared with 25% of white Americans. 20% of African Americans are uninsured compared to 12% of white Americans; [and] 24% of African Americans are covered by public insurance (Medicaid) as compared with 16% of white Americans.*" [12]

In 2011, Richard Allen Williams outlined five principles for eliminating racial disparities as part of healthcare reform: 1) Provide insurance coverage and access to high-quality care for all Americans, 2) Promote a diverse healthcare workforce, 3) Deliver patient-centered care, 4) Maintain accurate and complete race and ethnicity data to monitor disparities in care, 5) Set measurable goals for improving quality of care ensure that goals are achieved equitably for all racial and ethnic groups. Despite this ambitious plan, one must remember that access to financial resources is key to achieving healthcare independence which in many minority communities is obsolete.

African-Americans barriers to healthcare include the negative affect of environment or community, finances or lack of insurance a lack of medical practices associated with race history. (Ravenell, Whitaker, Johnson, 2008; Watson, 2014). Center to the debates now revolve around President's champion healthcare policy termed Affordable Care Act or (ACA), commonly known as Obamacare, which will eliminate barriers to obtaining healthcare. Through the ACA policy many under-represented groups now have access to health insurance coverage, with the aim of improving their access to utilization of healthcare. The number of people uninsured has reached an alarming rate and continues to drive many of the healthcare disparities among minority groups. The ACA will allow previously uninsured Americans to gain access to health insurance and may particularly benefit vulnerable populations. Yet despite this great public policy, financial burden become imperative on those who can afford the healthcare plans and thus money becomes a key asset on those who can or cannot afford ACA. See Figure 5 below.

Figure 5. Unisured by the Ethnic Races 2013-14

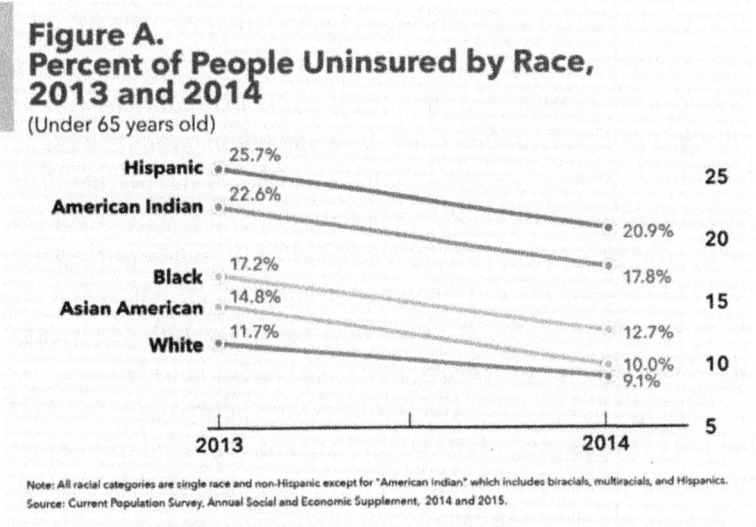

Source: Annual Social and Economic Supplement report. 2014-015

Figure 5 shows changes in the number of uninsured people by race, the access to the ACA and its impact on minority groups in 2014. The decline in uninsured was greatest among African-Americans and Hispanics, who traditionally have had the highest uninsured rates. For African-Americans, the uninsured rates decreased from *"17.2% in 2013 to 12.7% in 2014, while Hispanics went from 25.7% in 2013 to 20.9% in 2014, a decline of 5%, whereas whites only decreased of 2.6% during the same time period."* [13] Despite the reduction in the uninsured population, the number of people who remain without healthcare insurance continues to be disproportionally high among the ethnic minority groups. We witness the consequences to the uninsured: poor healthcare and little or no access to healthcare providers. Still, we can all agree that The Affordable Care Act has substantially reduced the number of Americans not having healthcare insurance and has increased access to quality healthcare for millions of people.

According to a recent study by Timothy Creedon at Brandeis University and Benjamin Lê Cook at the Health Equity Research Lab at Cambridge Health Alliance *"The ACA has not yet, however, helped ease racial disparities within behavioral health, with most of the significant gains in treatment coming for white patients. In other words, while white patients with behavioral-health issues and minorities with behavioral health-issues gained insurance coverage at similar rates, only white patients saw that increased coverage resulted in significantly better behavioral- and mental-health treatment."* [14] In part what the ACA has done is give a new voice to uninsured Americans. The ACA is a still much debated political topic today.

Though not perfect, the public policy afforded by the ACA has led to the closing of the largest gap among racial minorities, including poverty and education. It has extended healthcare coverage to many who were disfranchised from the healthcare system allowed them the opportunity to gain access to many of the treatments that have been lacking in their communities.

Healthcare Cost:

Central to the debates surrounding the disparities in our healthcare system is the financial capacity of individuals to afford the basic necessity of life; that is the monetary cost of having health insurance. The Kaiser Foundation report on Disparities in Healthcare concluded that *"Many groups are at disproportionate risk of being uninsured, lacking access to care experiencing worse health outcomes, including people of color and low-income individuals. Hispanics, Blacks, American Indians/Alaska Natives low-income individuals are more likely to be uninsured relative to Whites and those with higher incomes. Low-income individuals and people of color also face increased barriers to accessing care; receive poorer quality care experience worse health outcomes."* [15] They also concluded that low-income individuals also experience more barriers to care and receive poorer quality care than high-income individuals. Lesbian, gay, bisexual transgender (LGBT) individuals are more likely to experience challenges obtaining care than heterosexuals. Because of high health insurance deductibles, approximately 23 percent of Americans ages 19 to 64 were considered underinsured in the Kaiser report. This amounts to 31 million Americans who refuse to fill essential prescriptions, undergo necessary medical tests or procedures, or see doctors out of fear that doing so would leave them in a financial crisis. In fact, many choose to remain uninsured due to the lack of financial resources regardless of their health concerns simply put it, it's too expensive to be sick.

A report released by the Commonwealth Fund, a private foundation that conducts independent research on health and social issues found that *"in the past decade, health benefits for employed people have become less comprehensive. Companies are saddled with increasing health insurance premiums, which has meant employees, are forced to take on higher deductibles. Rates of underinsurance among Americans who receive health benefits through their employers climbed from 10 percent in 2003 to 20 percent in 2012 through 2014, according to the report."*[16] As a result of this continuing disparities, the government policy of ACA was aimed at eliminating the financial burden placed on many Americans who simply could not afford basic healthcare insurance or access to healthcare services due to their financial status. The ACA was passed into law by Congress to ease the burden of Americans who could not afford nor were on any healthcare coverage, thus making it affordable to all. It ensures that Americans with low and moderate income have access to quality health care, since it requires all Americans to have health insurance starting this year, or face financial penalties. The law expands Medicaid eligibility (in the states that have agreed to do so) to the poorest Americans *"those making up to 133% of the federal poverty line. It also provides* financial assistance for those making up to 400% of the poverty level to help them buy private insurance from state health exchanges." [17] Implementing the ACA began to reduce the rates of uninsured among the ethnic races and low income family as depicted by Figure 6 below.

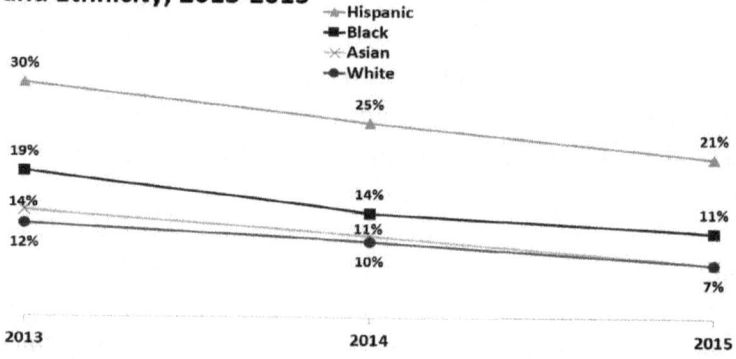

Figure 7
Uninsured Rates for the Nonelderly Population by Race and Ethnicity, 2013-2015

Source: Kaiser Foundation report on Healthcare Disparities. 2013-15

Figure 6 shows the declining rates of uninsured Americans. Access to insurance coverage is one of the major factors that contributed to racial and ethnic disparities prior to the government's mandated healthcare policy or ACA. The survey shows that racial and ethnic disparities in access have been reduced significantly during the first years of the ACA and it also expanded the accessibility for individuals to obtain healthcare coverage. Despite the success, the availability of federal subsidies to lower the cost of coverage in the ACA's Marketplaces has led to many individuals the inability to afford insurance coverage. Studies now show *"that almost a quarter of adults with private insurance had unaffordable coverage when premiums, deductibles total out-of-pocket costs were taken into account."*

No one will argue that the government healthcare program has not been both rebuked and praised. While implementation of the Affordable Care Act has led to unprecedented gains in health insurance coverage, it still remains a pivotal element in correcting the racial disparities that continue to exist among the races. Financial capacity to access the ACA become more imperative since the market rates fluctuates and at times makes it much more difficult to continue into the program despite what economic class you belong to.

Conclusion:
Disparities in healthcare remain rampant in today's society, brought about by the unequal treatment of people of color and supported by the public health policy and legislation based on discrimination. (Kirkham & Anderson, 2002) The underlying causes can be linked to socioeconomic differences which are the most significant factors in healthcare inequalities. Racial and ethnic minorities are more likely than whites to live in segregated, high-poverty communities that have historically suffered from a lack of quality healthcare.

Improving healthcare quality and reducing disparities among racial and ethnic minority groups requires an effort by both government and the healthcare industry, including drugs companies. The ACA is only beneficial to the extent in which it is used by everyday researchers, educators, healthcare providers Americans to change policy and improve culturally competent healthcare including patient education, screening procedures and access to healthcare for all minority groups.

About the Contributing Author:

Mrs. Rose Adams, MSN, RN, CPNP, is a PhD candidate in the Department of Nursing at Texas Woman's University. She received her Bachelors of Science and Masters of Science in Nursing at the University of Texas in Arlington. Mrs. Rose Adams currently serves as an Adjunct Professor of Nursing at Texas Christian University and currently resides in Fort Worth, Texas with her husband and two children.

Bibliography:
1. Agency for Healthcare Research and Quality (AHRQ). (2011). Disparities in healthcare quality among racial and ethnic minority groups: Selected finding from the 2010 National Healthcare Quality and Disparities Report. http://www.ahrq.gov/research/findings/nhqrdr/nhqrdr10/minority.html
2. Agency for Healthcare Research and Quality (AHRQ). (2014). National Healthcare Disparities Report, 2013 (AHRQ Publication No. 14-0006). Retrieved from http://www.ahrq.gov/research/findings/nhqrdr/nhdr13/2013nhdr.pdf
3. Center for Disease Control and Prevention (CDC). (2012). CDC Vital signs: Breast cancer. Retrieved from http://www.cdc.gov/vitalsigns/breastcancer/index.html
4. Center for Disease Control (CDC). (2011). CDC health disparities & inequalities report: United States. Retrieved from http://www.cdc.gov/Features/dsREACHUS/
5. Burris, H. & Collins, J. (2010). Race and preterm birth--the case for epigenetic inquiry. Ethnicity & Disease, 20(3), 296-299.
6. Kochanek K., Arias, E., & Anderson, R. (2013). How did cause of death contribute to racial differences in life expectancy in the United States in 2010? (NCHS data brief, no 125) Hyattsville, MD: National Center for Health Statistics.
7. MacDorman, M. and Mathews, T. (2011). NCHS Presentation to the Board of Scientific Counselors: Understanding Racial and Ethnic Disparities in U.S. Infant Mortality Rates. Retrieved from ttp://www.cdc.gov/nchs/data/bsc/bsc_Marian_MacDorman.pdf
8. Policy statement---Health equity and children's rights. (2010). Pediatrics, 125(4), 838-849. doi:10.1542/peds.2010-0235

9. Purnell, L. (2002). The Purnell Model for Cultural Competence. Journal of Transcultural Nursing, 13(3), 193-196.
10. Ravenell, J., Whitaker, E., & Johnson, W. J. (2008). According to him: barriers to healthcare among African-American men. Journal of the National Medical Association, 100(10), 1153-1160.
11. Siegel, S., Moy, E., Burstin, H. (2004). Assessing the nation's progress toward elimination of disparities in healthcare: The National Healthcare Disparities Report. Journal of General Internal Medicine, 19(2):195-200.
12. United States Department of Health and Human Services, Healthy People 2020. (2011, June 29). Immunization and Infectious Disease. Retrieved from http://www.healthypeople.gov/2020/topics-objectives/topic/immunization-and-infectious-diseases/objectives
13. Xu, J., Kochanek, K. D., Murphy, S. L., & Tejada-Vera, B. (2010). Deaths: final data for 2007. National Vital Statistics Reports: From The Centers for Disease Control and Prevention, National Center For Health Statistics, National Vital Statistics System, 58(19), 1-19.

References:
1. Peter Bach, New England Journal of Medicine. 2004
2. American Medical Association Report. Healthcare Disparities 2013
3. Ibid
4. American Medical Association Report. Healthcare Disparities 2013
5. Ibid
6. United States Census Bureau, 2012
7. http://www.cbsnews.com/news/when-health-care-is-equal-blacks-fare-better-than-whites/
8. http://www.cdc.gov/nchs/data/hus/hus15.pdf
9. https://www.heart.org/idc/groups/heart-
10. http://scholar.harvard.edu/files/nkc/files/2014_cv_disparities_current_cardiology_reports.pdf
11. x.http://ac.els-cdn.com/S016752731301944X/1-s2.0-S016752731301944X-main.pdf?_tid=22c38858-aa74-11e6-ab13-00000aab0f02&acdnat=1479132825_433befda76cc61f6716803feae5e48c6
xi. Horner RD, Salazar W, Geiger HJ, et al. Changing healthcare professionals' behaviors to eliminate disparities in healthcare: What do we know? How might we proceed? Am J Manag Care. 2004; 10: SP12–SP19
xii. "The Consequences of Being Uninsured for African Americans," Gail C. Christopher
xiii. http://www.theatlantic.com/politics/archive/2016/08/affordable-care-act-mental-health-disparities/490220/
xvi. http://kff.org/disparities-policy/issue-brief/disparities-in-health-and-health-care-five-key-questions-and-answers/
xv. Ibid
xvi. http://www.newsweek.com/many-americans-insured-cant-afford-health-care-334624
xvii. HHS homepage
xviii. http://www.commonwealthfund.org/~/media/files/publications/issue-brief/2015/nov/1844_collins_how_high_is-americas_hlt_care_cost_burden_tb_v1.pdf.

Chapter 8
Hate Crimes

"After more than a decade of opposition and delay, we've passed inclusive hate crimes legislation to help protect our citizens from violence based on what they look like, who they love, how they pray or who they are." [1]
-President Barack Obama

Racism continues to bear its ugly face in many shapes, sizes, and forms, and has continue to define America's post-racial society well into the 21st century. In fact, hate crimes have been as synonymous with American history as apple pie. The Jim Crow era stemmed from racially-fueled American terrorism that continues to perpetuate itself in our society. This terrorism manifests itself in religious, gay, gender, and color hatred, and has only increased in a time where social media has replaced the overt racism synonymous with American history. No other time in America's great history has the idea of a post-racial society caught the eye of so many Americans. The emergence of an African-American Presidential candidate in 2008 fueled the debate regarding where race and hatred fit in American society. As Barack Obama continues into his presidency, hate crimes continue to escalate, and show us that America is not ready to have a constructive dialogue on race, despite the election of our country's first African-American President.

Defined by the Department of Justice, "*hate crimes are the violence of intolerance and bigotry, intended to hurt and intimidate someone because of their race, ethnicity, national origin, religious, sexual orientation, or disability. The purveyors of hate use explosives, arson, weapons, vandalism, physical violence, and verbal threats of violence to instill fear in their victims, leaving them vulnerable to more attacks and feeling alienated, helpless, suspicious and fearful.*" [2] According to the head of the NAACP, Cornell Williams Brooks, "*The level of hate crimes in this country has remained constant over years,*" "*We have to allocate resources to address these hate groups and these hate crimes. The fact of the matter is; the Justice Department underestimates the degree of hate crimes in this country because they have to rely on self-reporting. That is a challenge. And the fact that we have at least 200,000 to 300,000 hate crimes in a given year is unconscionable and inconsistent with our values as Americans.*" [3] Events in Charleston, South Carolina; Orlando, Florida; and other American cities continue to remind us that hatred, racism, and bigotry are still parts of our culture, and fuel much of the ignorance that defines who we are and what we claim to stand for: a nation that preaches tolerance and respect.

Historical Background:

The end of the Civil War brought extreme racial hatred against African-Americans; the freedoms bestowed upon African-Americans by the 13th, 14th, and 15th Amendments came at a huge price. These freedoms gave rise to America's first terrorist group, the Ku Klux Klan. As a result, fear and intimidation became part of both African-American culture, and American culture as a whole. In fact, the FBI has been investigating what are now called "hate crimes" against African-Americans as far back as World War I. The role of hate crimes took a new twist upon the passage of the Civil Rights Act of 1964. The lynching of African-Americans in the early 19th and 20th century became part of American culture.

Family events on Sundays became a tradition closely associated with the lynching of an African-American; these events were commonly referred to as "picnics." According to the report, "*Lynching in America: Confronting the Legacy of Racial Terror,*" "*Lynchings were violent and public acts of torture that traumatized black people throughout the country and were largely tolerated by state and federal officials;*" the report's summary states: "*These lynchings were terrorism.*" [4] Ultimately, this report brings the magnitude of hate crimes against African-Americans into perspective, and elucidates the scope of these brutal hate crimes during the decades between Reconstruction and the Civil Rights era.

Missouri Congressman Leonidas Dyer first introduced his Anti-Lynching Bill--known as the Dyer Bill--into Congress in 1918. Despite not being included in the legislative halls of the nation's capital, the NAACP and the New Negro Movement of the Harlem Renaissance continued to push for legislation with the hope of addressing America's earliest hate crimes. Anti-Lynching legislation's passage became one of the NAACP's core goals, statistics of the time supported the NAACP's increased urgency in the anti-lynching campaign. According to the NAACP report, more than 1,200 blacks were lynched in the South between 1901 and 1929. Forty-one percent of these lynchings occurred in two exceptionally violent states: Georgia (250) and Mississippi (245)[5]. In 1935, another anti-lynching bill was introduced to congress, but little discussion took place and the bill died in the halls of congress. According to Professor Harvard Sitkoff, "In the end, was the cause of an anti-lynching bill simply subsumed by the Civil Rights Act of the 1960s?" [6]

The 21st Century:
In January 2009, much of the world watched America swear in its first African-American President, and hoped that America was willing to move past its ugly history and towards a post racial society. People dreamed of a more tolerable na-

tion that would fulfill Dr. Martin L. King's dream. Our expectations that America would transcend race, bigotry, ignorance, and hate crimes, and that both white and black racial attitudes would undergo a fundamental change, has not come to fruition. America's first African-American President and First Family have NOT alleviated racial stereotypes, hatred, and bigotry, nor have they engaged in any constructive dialogue on race and racism in America.

A recent Gallup poll, dated July 17, 2013, about Racial and Ethnic Relations in U.S. asked the question, *"Do you think that race relations between whites and blacks will always be a problem?"* About 40% of Americans said that race and black-white relations will always be a problem in the United States. Comparatively, when Gallup asked the same question in 1964, about 42% of Americans believed that race and black-white relations would always be a problem in the United States. [7] These statistics clearly illustrate that very little, if any, progress has occurred in the last fifty years when it comes to race relations. According to the FBI, *"Investigating hate crimes is the number one priority of our Civil Rights program. Why? Not only because hate crimes have a devastating impact on families and communities, but also because groups that preach hatred and intolerance plant the seeds of terrorism here in our country."* [8]

According to a report released by the Southern Poverty Law Center (SPLC), a prominent Civil Rights organization based in Montgomery, Alabama, the number of domestic hate and extremist groups in the United States grew to record levels in 2011. This growth was led by a surge in anti-government radicalism. In 2011 America had 1,018 "hate groups" nationwide, representing a slight increase from the previous record, 2010, when America had 1,002 hate groups.

See Figure 1 below.

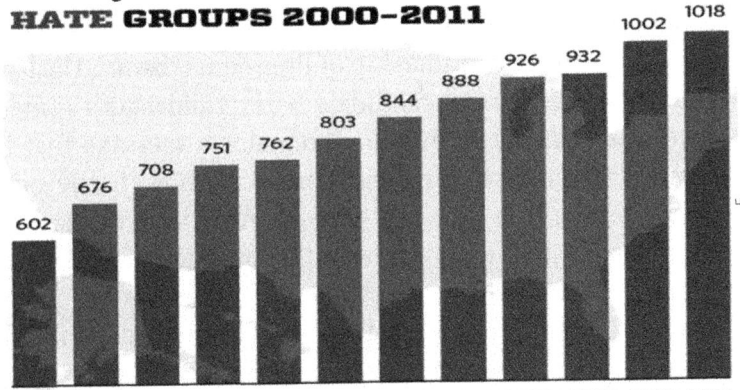

Source: Southern Poverty Law Center 2012 Report.

This continued increased directly coincides with the election of the nation's first African-American President, which led to increased hatred and bigotry against people of color and homosexuals.

According to a Huffington Post report, *"perhaps more disturbing than the small, yet sustained rise in hate groups, is the parabolic growth over the last few years in the number of anti-government "Patriot" and militia groups reported by the SPLC. These groups, which are categorized separately from hate groups, grew 55% to 1,274 in 2011, up from 824 in 2010. In 2008 such groups totaled only 149, while in 2009 the total increased to 512."* [9] See Figure 2 below.

Source: Southern Poverty Law Center 2012 Report.

The SPLC attributes these increases to widespread hatred and radicalism in addition to the frustration towards government policies and the leadership of President Obama. The late Senator and Presidential candidate Barry Goldwater's coined phrase, *"Can't Legislate Morality,"* remains a message that is lost in today's society. The racist American mind frame cannot change; the idea that post-Obama America will become the melting pot that we are constantly reminded of, and often embrace, remains a distant dream.

While hate groups in the United States have declined in the last 5 years, the hate crime rate remains steady, and crimes against African-Americans still lead all racially motivated crimes. Recent hate crimes in Florida, California, and other parts of the country reinforce the racist attitudes that haunt our diverse society. Whether these crimes are racially, religiously, or gender motivated, they take away the best of who we are and what we can become as a nation.

See Figure 3 below.

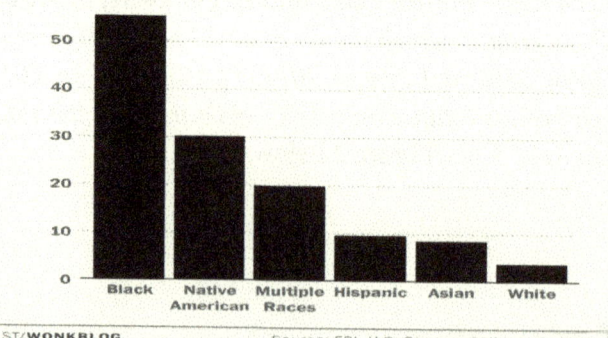

Source. The Washington Post

African-Americans still experience a higher rate of hate crimes than any other ethnic group in America. The increased rate of crime African-Americans experience stems from systematic hatred that perpetrates all avenues of life in many African-American communities. With the advent of social media, ignorance continues to replace overt hate groups, such as the KKK and the White Camelia Groups. Social media provides many hate groups with an easy method of advocating their racism and promoting their dangerous ignorance.

Is Gay Rights a Civil Rights Issue?

Recent, deadly attacks against the LBGT community have stirred the conscious of our nation, yet the debate about whether gay rights has become a Civil Rights issue continues to linger. Would Dr. King endorse the gay rights agenda, and would gay rights become the new Civil Rights issue of the 21st century? These intriguing, but complicated, questions have left many Civil Rights activists of the 1960's lost as they confront America's new Civil Rights agenda. Regardless of the debates, gay rights are a divisive issue that have our nation scrambling for an identity of tolerance. Matthew Shepheard's death has stirred the nation's conscience on the brutality that is synonymous with gay hate crimes. On October 28, 2009, over eleven years after Shepard's murder, President Barack Obama signed into law the Matthew Shepard and James Byrd Jr. Hate Crimes Prevention Act. The Shepard/Byrd Act gave the Department of Justice the power to investigate and prosecute bias-motivated violent crimes against LGBT victims, quite similar to the Civil Rights Act of 1964.

According to ABC news *"In Boston, Bishop Gilbert Thompson does not like it one bit 'I resent that homosexuals are trying to piggy back on the civil rights struggles of the 60's,' in Los Angeles, the Rev. Lee Peterson says 'it's offensive that the civil rights movement is not about sex.' In Chicago, Detroit and Raleigh, NC black ministers are beginning to preach on an uncomfortable subject in African-American circles, gay marriage, they argue has no place in a movement defined by Jim Crow laws and the right to vote."* [10]

Justice Clarence Thomas, the only African-American justice in the US Supreme court, concurs with many of the African-American clergy that gay rights should not be defined as a Civil Rights issue. In Obergefell vs. Hodges, Thomas – the second black jurist to serve in the Supreme Court's 226-year history – unleashed a scathing dissent in the same-sex marriage case, "*rejecting the notion that gays, like African-Americans, had suffered from second-class citizenship. Unlike slaves, he argued, lacking the right to marry didn't prevent gays from traveling freely across state lines, or subject them to overt discrimination.*"[11] Justice Thomas further elaborates on his views by stating that, "*The corollary of that principle is that human dignity cannot be taken away by the government. Slaves did not lose their dignity (any more than they lost their humanity) because the government allowed them to be enslaved. Those held in internment camps did not lose their dignity because the government confined them. And those denied governmental benefits certainly do not lose their dignity because the government denies them those benefits.*"[12]

Yet, others argue the opposite, including the late Civil Rights activist Julian Bond who elaborated on CNN: *One of the most cynical things I've ever heard of or ever seen [is] the idea that black people who oppose gay marriage, black people who support gay marriage, can be moved around like pieces on a chess board - it's so scary.*"[13] He further concluded about the LBGT community that, "*We ought to be happy when other people, including gays and lesbians and many other people, have imitated the black movement for human rights. They've adopted our songs: we ought to be happy. They've adopted out slogans, we ought to be happy. They've adopted the way in which we went about it, in a non-violent way, generally speaking: we ought to be proud of that, that we served as an example to others. And when others imitate what we did, to gain their rights, we ought to be first in line to say, 'Can I help you?'*"[14] The general message of his argument is that hatred is hatred; ignorance is ignorance; and bigotry is bigotry, and that all these ideas have no place in American society.

In fact, the point of Civil Rights Movement of the 1960's was to eradicate these hatreds. In fact, the late Coretta Scott King, wife of Dr. Martin L. King, spent many years urging African-Americans and the black church to fulfill Dr. King's legacy by recognizing gay rights as a Civil-Rights issue. Congressman and Civil Rights activist John Lewis commented on this major debate, and remarked that *"I fought too hard and too long against discrimination based on race and color not to stand up and speak up against discrimination against our gay and lesbian brothers and sisters. I see the right to marriage as a civil rights issue."* [15] The lingering debate on Gay-Civil Rights has divided the nation with regard to what is civil or not. Many people, though, argue that discrimination is wrong in all forms: religious, racial, sexual, etc. In fact, throughout our Civil Rights history, gay activists and Civil Rights activist have had a close link. Famed author James Baldwin struggled with his sexuality as an African-American in the 1950's, and Bayard Rustin not only orchestrated the famed March on Washington in 1963, but was one of Dr. King's closest advisors in the Civil Rights Movement. Interestingly, they were both openly gay.

According to Mrs. Loretta Lynch, US Attorney General, the recent terrorist attack on a gay community in Orlando, Florida was *"'an act of hate and terror,' emphasizing that the lesbian, gay, bisexual and transgender community continues to be the target of attacks in this country."* [16] She further elaborated that *"We're moving quickly; we're trying to uncover everything we can about this killer's motivations, what led him to this particular place, this particular club,' Why did he target the LGBT community, a community that so often is the victim of hate crime, in both an act of hate and terror?"* [17] According to Mrs. Lynch, FBI statistics for 2015 showed a 67% increase in hate crimes against Muslim Americans. Hate crimes against Jewish people, African Americans, and LGBT individuals also increased. Overall, reported hate crimes spiked 6%, but the number could be higher because many incidents go unreported, Lynch said. "These numbers should be deeply sobering for all Americans.

President Trump and Gateway towards Hate:

The 2016 Presidential election has slowly but surely developed into a debate on the politics of hatred, bigotry, anti-immigrants, islamophobia, homophobic hatred, and the more so opening the flood gates of America's cancer; Racism. Never in American electoral history has a President exhibited so much division along races, class, and ethnic lines that it has become such an important part of the electoral process. President Donald Trump's racist remark reminds us that the hatred towards ethnic minorities is alive and well in a country that preaches integration and acceptance of all. It must be noted that racism has been alive and well prior to the election of the nation's 45th President, what he has done was simply awaking a sleeping giant that has been lurking in the waters of America.

The history of America has been closely pegged with racism and discrimination against African-Americans; it's an issue the country has struggled to address in every stage of the great nation. Our house of democracy has been plagued with cracks of racism and discrimination against African-Americans, women and other minority groups. During the last 300 years we have made little attempts to fix these cracks and as a result, we have struggled with defective a foundation that racism built. The recent elections have showed the vulnerability of these cracks and defective foundation, as result hatred and bigotry have continued to surface and perpetuate an unimaginable character of our nation that many refused to condemn.

According the New Yorker magazine, *"since Donald Trump won the Presidential election, there has been a dramatic uptick in incidents of racist and xenophobic harassment across the country. The Southern Poverty Law Center has reported that there* were four hundred and thirty-seven incidents of intimidation between the election, on November 8th, and November 14th, targeting blacks and other people of color, Muslims, immigrants, the L.G.B.T. community, and women." [18] The Southern Poverty Law Center, a non-profit center that tracks racial hatred, combat domestic extremism, and race based crimes concluded that resident-elect Donald Trump's win calling it a "new reality." "Today, we're facing a new reality – a president-elect who has denigrated people because of their race, their religion, their ethnicity, their gender, and more," SPLC President Richard Cohen wrote. "Our mission is to hold Donald Trump to what he is saying now –that he will be a president for all Americans and that he will work to bind the wounds of division, wounds that his own words have caused." [19] Hidden white supremacists have felt that they now have a voice in their hatred in an ever changing ethnic, diverse America. As a result of the President's rhetoric during his campaign this voice has come to fruition and racial hatred and backlash have now been given a free pass to individual that don't look American or for those who feel that they don't have a rightful place in America.

Recent islamophobia remarks by the newly elected President of the free world has left many religious groups fearful of practicing the religious beliefs in a country that champions separation of church and state. According to experts at the Anti-Defamation League and the Southern Poverty Law Center who monitor hate groups and anti-Muslim sentiment, "Trump's call on Monday to halt the entrance of Muslims to the United States is driving online chatter among white supremacists and is likely to inspire violence against Muslims." [20]

Conclusion:

Civil Rights has always been the beacon of hope in America, how we treat and respect people despite their differences has always been the measure of our democracy. Yet despite this constitutional and moral obligation, modern day anti-Civil

Rights rhetoric continue to define who we are and what we stand for as a nation that preaches democracy. Hate crimes despite what format or elements it embodies has taken away the best of who we are and what we can become as a nation that preaches tolerance and acceptance. Whether we admit or not, hatred is hatred despite what format it takes, homophobic, religious hatred, immigrant hatred, etc. Hate crimes has continued to define who we are as a nation that preached tolerance and diversity but is still filled with hatred and bigotry.

References:
1. http://www.politico.com/story/2009/10/obama-signs-hate-crimes-bill-into-law-028866
2. https://www.justice.gov/crs/hate-crime
3. http://www.cbsnews.com/news/face-the-nation-transcripts-june-21-2015-brooks-scott-nunes/
4. https://www.washingtonpost.com/news/post-nation/wp/2015/02/10/even-more-black-people-were-lynched-in-the-u-s-than-previously-thought-study-finds/?utm_term=.ad59a4c859ef
5. The NAACP report, Thirty Years of Lynching in the United States, 1889–1919
6. http://www.npr.org/templates/story/story.php?storyId=4701576
7. Gallup Poll Race Relations, July 17th 2013 http://www.gallup.com/poll/163535/americans-rate-racial-ethnic-relations-positively.aspx
8. https://www.fbi.gov/about-us/investigate/civilrights/hate_crimes
9. http://www.huffingtonpost.com/brian-levin-jd/hate-groups-splc_b_1331318.html
10. http://abcnews.go.com/WNT/story?id=131679
11. http://www.usnews.com/news/articles/2015/06/26/thomas-no-link-between-civil-rights-and-gay-rights
12. Ibid
13. http://www.dailykos.com/story/2015/7/21/1404428/-Julian-Bond-Gay-rights-are-civil-rights
14. Ibid
15. http://www.npr.org/2015/07/02/419554758/african-americans-question-comparing-gay-rights-movement-to-civil-rights
16. http://www.huffingtonpost.com/entry/loretta-lynch-orlando-shooting_us_5766c3ace4b0853f8bf12eeb
17. Ibid

18. http://www.newyorker.com/news/news-desk/hate-on-the-rise-after-trumps-election
19. http://www.cnsnews.com/news/article/lauretta-brown/southern-poverty-law-center-facing-new-reality-calls-trump-advisers-far
20. http://www.politico.com/story/2015/12/donald-trump-white-supremacists-216620

Chapter 9
The Politics of Race, Immigration Reform, and the 2016 Presidential Election

> *"Scripture tells us that we shall not oppress a stranger, for we know the heart of a stranger-- we were strangers once, too. My fellow Americans, we are and always will be a nation of immigrants. We were strangers once, too."* [1]
> -President Barack Obama, November 20, 2014.

The 2016 Presidential election has slowly but surely developed into a debate on the politics of immigration reform and the courting of Hispanic electoral votes, never in American electoral history has an ethnic group become such an important part of the electoral process. Despite this importance, center to the debates is comprehensive immigration reform, the politics of race and the political impact of the new Americans or those we often refer to as undocumented immigrants.

Both Democrats and Republicans have acknowledged the importance of the Hispanic vote, and they approached the new voting sector more cautiously as the 2013 Immigration Reform bill becomes a stumbling policy for the potential presidential candidates. The Hispanic vote not only became a political weapon in 2012, but in 2016, their votes will dictate who will become the future leader of the free world. America's Hispanic population is the fastest growing segment during the last two decades, the U.S. Census Bureau in 2014 estimated that 1 in 6 Americans is Hispanics. This growth continues to increase with more arrivals on foreign born immigrants from mostly Latin American countries striving to achieve American citizenship. The Bureau also reported that during the last decade, Hispanics made up more than half of U.S. population growth, this growth will pose new socio-economic and political dilemma for America and its political parties.

According to Mary Waters and Karl Eschbach's Immigration and Ethnic and Racial Inequality in the United States. *"The new global order has changed the racial and ethnic map of the United States one further way. Immigration has had a very large impact on American society since the 1960s, and most especially it has increased the diversity of the nonwhite population of the United States. In 1990, 7.9% of the US population was foreign born. The 19.8 million foreign-born people in the United States is the largest number in US history. The sources of immigration flows have also shifted as a consequence of changes in immigration law and in the international pattern of migration flows. In 1990, 25.2% of the foreign-born population was Asian, 42.5% Latin American, 22% European, and 10.3% from other countries."* [2] The population shift during the last three decades has brought about a more diverse America, with a large and powerful new Hispanic population that can change the political landscape with their voting power and allegiance to either political party. The fundamental issue remains how can both Democrat and Republican Parties court the new Americans and how can they do it in a sensitive but compelling way?

The Politics of Race & Immigration:
The Hispanic presence in America dates back to the founding of this great nation, Hispanics have contributed in every avenue of American life since the inception of this great country. Many are unaware that Hispanic culture had firm roots in St Augustine, Florida and what is now New Mexico before the English arrived at Jamestown and before the Pilgrims dropped anchor in Massachusetts Bay. The love- hate relationship with immigrants and America is as old as apple pie, Benjamin Franklin in 1753 warned of German immigrants overrunning America, and not only was he concerned about the increasing number of German immigrants, he worried that the German immigrants would threaten the Anglo-English language and insisted that America must set the principle of Anglo-conformity as the model of immigration. Samuel Huntington, who some argue was our first president under the Article of Confederation, once described brown skins Mexicans as savages and uncivilized. Interestingly, both gentlemen were signers of the Declaration of Independence, which preaches life, liberty and the purse of happiness.

Whether we admit it or not, many of our immigration laws and the politics behind them have been historically woven with racial prejudice against recent immigrants. Throughout history the U.S. immigration policies of welcoming other groups have been tainted with race-based policies, e.g., The Naturalization Act of 1790, which granted the rights of American citizenship to all *"free white persons";* and the Chinese Exclusion Act of 1882 which barred Chinese immigrants from becoming naturalized citizens. Moreover, the plight of Jewish immigrants and Jewish community in America has face discrimination from hateful slurs to barring of their ships in U.S. ports pre and post Holocaust years. These anti-immigration laws all helped shape and define our political history and the way we view outsiders in a land that was built by many of these ethnic groups.

President Donald Trump's racist remark reminds us that the hatred towards immigrants is alive and well in a country that preaches integration and acceptance of all. Very few Americans remember the historical racism that Mexican immigrants encountered in the early 1900's, then the U.S. Public Health Service (USPHS) in 1916 began implementing a series of anti-health laws targeted at Mexican immigrants crossing the U.S.–Mexico border. The health department and our government rationale was that Mexicans were bringing diseases into the United States, therefore American health policies had to change in order to secure the border and keep Mexicans out of America. Another example of racist remarks and policy directed towards Mexican immigrants occurred in the 1929 stock market crash. This event led to the greatest depression in American history, a time when one out four Americans was unemployed, our economy shattered and confidence in American idealism was tested. As many Americans suffered from the economic depression, Mexican immigrants became the scapegoat for America's economic, social, and political problems.

As a result, Mexican immigrants were denied jobs, subjected to raids, illegally arrested and detained without due process. As a result of this fear of immigrants, the American government between 1929 to 1939 deported some one to two million Mexican American citizens and legal residents of Mexican descent; this mass deportation was known as the Mexican Repatriation policy with the aim of cleansing America's ill. Mexican immigrants became the scapegoat for America's economic, social, political problems, these policies, along with other racist ideologies, continued to persist throughout the 1930's, 40's, 50's '60's and to the 21st century. According to

Garcia, Ruben J., Critical Race Theory and Proposition 187: The Racial Politics of Immigration Law. *"Undocumented immigrants provide a convenient scapegoat for the social problems currently confronting America, making anti-immigrant rhetoric prevalent and acceptable in politics today."* [3]

No other immigrant group in the history of our great nation has the potential to redefine America, whether economically, politically or socially, Hispanics have now become the cornerstone of the America's foundation. Despite this as we enter the 21st century, several questions remains where do Hispanics fit into the American society? How are Hispanics changing the face of the America, and can they redefine our political institution? What's the role can the comprehensive immigration reform play on the American political process in 2016 and future; will the American Presidency be dictated by the Hispanic vote?

The Debate:

The politics of race has never been so insightful that it has brought the worst out of us, and what America can become as a great diverse society. Immigration has always been the basic DNA of nation and it has taken away the best of who we are and what we can become as an immigrant nation. Current immigration reform laws has more implications for America's future than many of us can foresee; not only socially, culturally and economically, but Hispanic political presence, is already shaping and defining a new American political landscape. The political debacle of the current immigration debate has left the United States of America divided along racial, ethnic and political lines never seen before in our great country. Not only has the debate gone beyond the boundaries of our political spectrum, it has left the American people and America's political parties scrambling to maintain a sense of what true democracy can be. As both political parties delve into the murky depths of the current immigration debate, they have ignored the fact that we are an immigrant nation, who we are as Americans and more so the political implications on the *"Browning of America."*

The Comprehensive Immigration reform policies are directly related to the future of America, both to the American people, but more so to the political parties as they try to court America's greatest asset--The Hispanic Vote. The Immigration debate has now generated so many divisions in our society that it has become the *"Civil Rights debate of 21st Century."* Never in American history has immigration been such a decisive issue where policymaking and the electoral process go hand in hand.

As both political parties implement their 2016 political agendas, they are facing an increasingly tough decision whether or not to support a comprehensive Immigration Reform bill that will define the future American President. Both parties have acknowledged the importance of the Hispanic vote, and they have approached the new voting sector more cautiously as the 2013 Immigration Reform bill becomes a stumbling domestic policy for the potential presidential candidates. Very few candidates have addressed immigration reform with any constructive dialogue or solutions, and even those who have addressed immigration have doomed themselves to failure in the eyes of many Hispanics electorates.

Their decision will ultimately lead to a backlash from their own constituents and those of favor or impede efforts to provide a path to citizenship for undocumented immigrants living in America. The political importance of the Hispanic vote is closely tied to Immigration reform and, whether or not we admit it, **the American Presidency will be dictated by the Hispanic vote.** This vote, which can be utilized by both political parties, will now define the American political process and who or which party controls America's future political landscape.

Since 2010 the number of Hispanic eligible voters has increased by some 3.9 million. Their share among eligible voters nationally is also on the rise, the 2014 elections, the Hispanic electorate accounted for 11% of total voters, up from 10.1% in 2010 and 8.6% in 2006, reflecting the relatively faster growth of the Hispanic electorate compared with other groups. Both political parties have redefined their political agenda to cater to the Hispanics' ever growing presence. Politically their votes remain hugely important for both Democratic and Republican campaigns. Both the Democrats and Republicans have agreed that the Hispanic immigration agenda must be dealt in a very sensitive but cautious way, and their votes will define America's political landscape.

According to Senator Lindsey Graham (R) *"If we don't pass immigration reform, if we don't get it off the table in a reasonable, practical way, it doesn't matter who you run in 2016. We're in a demographic death spiral as a party, and the only way we can get back in good graces with the Hispanic community, in my view, is pass comprehensive immigration reform."* [v] The Democratic Party argues, *"Hispanics are a swing vote; they are no longer a base vote of our party. Though we can all agree that it is the democratic agenda that will help Hispanics live a better life, we need to tell them in a compelling way. When we speak to them we can move them our way; they can break the Republican Party."* [5]

The Republican Party also acknowledged the political importance of the Hispanic vote, *"given the size, growth rate and the distribution of Hispanics, it is safe to say that if we do not respect their voting power, they can change the future of elections."* [vii] Whatever the debates are both political parties must be vigilant on how we secure their votes, in fact, according to Janet Murguia, President of the National Council of La Raza, *"The road to the White House runs right through the Hispanic community, and you will not see a Republican become president without it."* [viii]

As the debates over immigration reform continue to evolve into a political debacle, the Immigration Reform bill focuses mostly on three issues: the economic effects of legalizing millions of currently illegal immigrants as well as all future immigration; the possibility of achieving real border security; and the ethical question of offering the reward of citizenship to those who have entered the country illegally. Despite this, the political implication on America's future and the Hispanic vote remains critical to the survival of American democracy. The underlying truth remains: despite what roles the Democratic and Republican parties play in comprehensive immigration reform, it will have an important future impact on which political party assumes control of the White House. Hispanics, a swing vote demographic, will align themselves with a party that will cater to their needs, their votes will dictate the future of America, and this decision will ultimately define the future of the political landscape in America.

The Dilemma:

The growth of the Hispanic electorate will be an important factor in an increasing number of congressional races across the country in upcoming elections and beyond. More numbers mean more votes. Their presence is now swing votes in some 14 states and can increase to 16 states by the Presidential election of 2016. According to the 2013 American Progress report on the Growth of Latino Electorate in Key states, they concluded that *"given the Latino population's rapid growth its political influence will be greater in 2016 elections, over the next 4 years the Latino voters nationwide is projected to increase by 4 million people-an increase by 17%. The Latino community's influence is even more pronounced at the state level and key states where the growth of Latino eligible voters is outpacing all other groups."* [ix] This increased population growth along with immigration reform will bring more votes to the table, and how to attract these voters becomes a political chess game for both Democrats and Republicans.

Moreover, how both parties handle the issue of comprehensive immigration reform will have a serious impact on Hispanic political voting behavior in 2016 Presidential and future elections. The growing presence of the Hispanic community will have profound political consequence on each political party and future immigration reform policy will play an important part in defining America's new political process.

If the Immigration Reform bill were to pass, what would be the implications on our political landscape? The new law will allow unauthorized immigrants to gain eventual citizenship but also carries electoral risks and rewards for both Republican and Democratic Parties. On the one hand, if the bill were passed, its paves the way for new voters but more important which political party will they align themselves with? According to Nate Silver, *"roughly 80 percent of illegal immigrants are Hispanic, and about 10 percent are Asian, both groups that voted heavily Democratic in the last two elections. On the other hand, such legislation could plausibly improve the Republican Party's brand image among Hispanics and Asian-Americans, perhaps allowing the party to fare better among these voters in future elections."* [x] These immigration changes will have a long term effect on our political process: they would affect the status of the 11 million unauthorized immigrants who are already in the United States who will eventually become U.S. Citizens and exercise one of the fundamental rights we have in America; the right to vote.

According to the Congressional Budget Office, if the Immigration Reform bill becomes law, it will add more than 17 million new potential voting-age citizens by 2036. These potential voters are in addition to the nearly 15 million that the current level of legal immigration will add by 2036. Combined, current immigration would add more than 32 million potential new voting-age citizens by 2036. [xi] These changing political demographics paint an alarming political fiasco that neither political party can afford to underestimate. If the bill becomes law, Hispanic youths and naturalized immigrants will be 34 percent of newly eligible voters in 2014, 35 percent in 2016, 36 percent in 2018, and 37 percent in 2020. [xii] California will experience the greatest impact of the Immigration Reform bill, with nearly two-thirds of newly eligible voters belonging to either Hispanic or Asians. The same effect will take place in many other states where the voting power will be held by swing votes in both current and future elections. States like New Mexico, Texas, Florida, Virginia, North Carolina, Colorado, New York, New Jersey and Nevada will now have an important and decisive Hispanic vote that will dictate the future of elections and political parties.

On other hand, if the bill fails, political consequences can undermine the future of both parties and in the long run might be a death sentence for the party that opposes immigration reform. Political parties may become extinct if they don't cater to the Hispanic needs and concerns. How they attract and court the new Hispanic voters can be a compelling, cautious and sensitive issue. According to the 2013 Gallup Poll, *"Hispanic-Americans favor Democrats over Republicans by a roughly 2-to-1 margin. Second generation Hispanic-Americans were actually more likely to identify with either party than Hispanic immigrants. Sixty-four percent of Hispanics who were born in the U.S. to parents who were also born in the U.S. favor Democrats, while only 30 percent lean Republican. Hispanic immigrants favor Democrats over Republicans by a margin of 57 to 25. And among Hispanics born in the U.S. to at least one immigrant parent, 57 percent lean Democratic, while 34 percent lean Republican."* [xiii] The Republican Party has already acknowledged that to win back the American presidency, they must make enormous gains in the Hispanic community, a voting bloc that only committed 27% of their votes to the Republicans in 2012 presidential election. This backlash was solely based on the self-deportation policy the Republican Party took on the immigration issue, which *infuriated* the Hispanic voting bloc. The Democratic Party prides itself as the party for Hispanics, yet they have failed to deliver any sought of immigration reform that is meaningful to secure the loyalty of the Hispanic vote. Failure to deliver a sensible Comprehensive Immigration Reform bill might spell death and allegiance of the Hispanic vote for both political parties in 2016 Presidential and future elections.

Both parties must be cautious and reflect on California's Proposition 187, an anti-immigrant policy which outlawed affirmative action and bilingual programs in the early 1990s and its long term effect on the Republican Party that sponsored the legislation. At a time when the Hispanic electoral was only 10% of the state population, this anti-immigrant policy began to mobilize California's Hispanic community, and by 2012 some 70% of Hispanics identified with the Democratic Party. Hispanics not only began taking part in the electoral process but voted heavily Democratic; this anti-immigrant policy awoke the sleeping giant in California--- the Hispanic vote. California's political landscape was never the same and became heavily democratic as a result of Proposition 187 anti-immigrant policy directed towards Hispanics. Not only did the mobilization of the Hispanic vote in California destroy the relationship with the Republican Party, it cost them an important voting bloc for future elections.

Some 20 years after Proposition 187, Hispanics are California's largest voting bloc and the political representation in the state has since doubled among their legislators. Can this effect be a new national dilemma facing both Democrats and Republicans, can the Hispanic vote be closely tied the Immigration Reform bill, can the future of both parties afford not to please the Hispanic swing votes? These questions rest solely on the importance of both political parties and how they court America's growing important swing votes. Neither political party can afford to play with the Hispanic vote; immigration reform is a key tool to courting America's greatest political asset. How both political parties resolve the immigration debacle can be an important gauge on the future of American political process, political activist, Presidential hopeful, and businessman Donald Trump remarked, *"Immigration reform is a suicide mission for GOP."* [xiv]

The courting of the Hispanic, African-American and women votes have never been an important element of the Republican Party, however both parties need to embrace the new American citizens with great admiration and respect. Face the Nations' Bob Schieffer reminded us the Republicans *"are old white men and they are dying."* [xv] The Democratic Party must also respect and acknowledge the growing importance of this voting bloc, they must speak to them in a cautious but meaningful way, their votes are not guaranteed to any one political party.

The Need for Comprehensive Immigration Reform:

The Comprehensive Immigration Reform debate goes far beyond the typical immigration debates on loss of jobs, drain on our social system, criminals etc., it has now vested in *"Building a Wall."* The economic, political, and social clout of current immigrants is far more beneficial to the nation than our media critics and politicians point them out to be. This complicated but imperative public policy must be achieved by the new Presidential administration for a number of reasons. Yet it must be also done in a sensitive and compelling way that make us Americans with a humanistic approach.

First and foremost, Comprehensive Immigration Reform must be done in a humanistic way that makes us a nation that still champions human rights. As the leader democratic free world, our history reminds us of our vast atrocities of human rights violations; Slavery, Trail of Tears, Mexican Repatriation Act, and last but definitely not least Japanese Internment, is American history is doomed to repeat itself? Human rights becomes the center of the debates, families that have lived here undocumented for decades, children who grew up in American communities, established friends and community relationships must take a humanism precedents than our harsh political rhetoric suggest. We must be cautious and vigilant on how we plan to address America's greatest resource--immigrants; it must be done with a humanistic approach, one filled with love and compassion. The breaking up and removal of families who have solidified their roots here is un-American, un-Constitutional and it is not what we stand for as a country that preaches tolerance, diversity and acceptance.

As we delve into the deep waters of American patriotism, the backlash that many of the undocumented immigrants are unpatriotic towards America's culture and refused to be American. One would question what is or not to be American? This debate has not only generated dialogue about the continued role that Americanism play in our society, but has also posed the question of whether undocumented immigrants are truly committed to the *"Land of the free and the home of the brave."* The issue should NOT be whether undocumented immigrants are loyal to America, that question was answered when undocumented men and women signed up and served in our military, fighting to protect and promote democracy throughout the world. It must be noted that some 38,000 military officials serving in both Iraq & Afghanistan Wars were not American citizens. In fact, history has forgotten that Lance. Cpl. Jose Gutierrez became one of the first casualty in Iraq, yes he did come to America illegally and died serving America's cause. Hence, the question is not whether undocumented immigrants are loyal to America, but whether America has lived up to its rich tradition of welcoming immigrants in a fair and impartial way?

Secondly, the debate has turned to the economic impact of these undocumented immigrants on American society. These economic arguments has been debunked by many economic pundits on the grounds that undocumented immigrants do not undercut wages, nor are they a drain on social services, and the fact they don't take jobs that would otherwise go to Americans. The majority of undocumented immigrants are unskilled and thus never pose any economic competition for skilled jobs that are secure by legal residents or American citizens. In fact, economists have stated that undocumented workers actually compliment the economy and it's the driving force behind our economic growth and prosperity. An interesting report released by the Social Security Administration in 2013, Stephen Goss, Chief Actuary for the Office, claimed that undocumented workers contribute about $15 billion a year to Social Security through payroll taxes. On the flip side, Goss also commented that these undocumented immigrants only receive about $1 billion since many of them are not eligible to receive benefits that they paid into. What is more astonishing, Goss noted in an interview for the New York Times, articulated that undocumented immigrants have contributed up to $300 billion, or nearly 10 percent, of the $2.7 trillion of the nation's Social Security Trust Fund. In other words, the benefits far out reach many of the critics of undocumented immigrants. The need to reach a humane solution on the immigration nightmare will ultimately benefit all. Hence, there is a need to create a legal path to 12 million residents enabling them to come out of the shadows of despair and allow them to continue contribute to the American economic pie in a fair and just way.

Last and by no means least, center to argument is the breaking and outright disregard of our laws by undocumented immigrants, after all we are a nation of laws. I do concur with all Americans that laws are to be respected, acknowledged, and obeyed by all. As American patriot, Reverend, and Civil Rights activist Dr. Martin L. King noted that there are two types of laws: just laws and unjust laws. Dr. King further elaborated one has not only a legal but a moral responsibility to obey just laws, *"but conversely, one has a moral responsibility to disobey unjust laws."* I must remind the American masses that Slavery, Racism, and Jim Crow segregation in our society was legal and Dr. King, his non-violence movement for Civil Rights, and the Abolitionist Movement in Southern states were considered illegal. Americans openly voiced their disgust on undocumented immigrants' willingness to break our laws, yet it becomes paradoxical in our society when we obey and dis-obey laws that are there to maintain law, order, and stability despite how ignorant they be. As long as we have double standards in our society, as long as our President Donald J. Trump and other billionaires insisted that they avoided paying taxes by merely exploiting tax loopholes legally, our legal integrity must be examined. As long as there are criticisms on undocumented immigrants for not paying their fair share of taxes but at the same time Americans remain silent on our President's 15 year non-payment of federal taxes, hence, we have the right to question the integrity of our laws.

Conclusion:

America is only great as the doors and opportunities we open to others, Comprehensive Immigration Reform matters because America matters. They go hand in hand and without each other, there can be no America. Success in America is not determined by our ethnic background or our native language but our commitment and dedication that is so much part of our past and present immigrants. American history will remind us that oppression takes away the best of who we are and what we can become as a nation founded on immigration. America's passion of including all that choose to come here has been to cornerstone of our democracy and constitutionalism, without this inclusiveness the American dream would not be possible.

Whatever the debates might be, neither party can afford to ignore nor play with the Hispanic vote. Immigration reform is a key tool to courting America's greatest political asset and the future of the American presidency. How and when both political parties address immigration reform remains a struggle; there must be a common-sense ideology on immigration reform by both the Democratic and Republican parties. There must be a sensible solution to the Civil Rights issue of the 21st century---immigration reform. Failure to do so and to court the Hispanic vote can lead to catastrophic alienation of both political parties and their future in American politics.

References:
1. President Obama Speech on Immigration Reform. November 20, 2014. https://www.whitehouse.gov/blog/2014/11/20/we-were-strangers-once-too-president-announces-new-steps-immigration
2. Mary Waters and Karl Eschbach's Immigration and Ethnic and Racial Inequality in the United States
3. Garcia, Ruben J., "Critical Race Theory and Proposition 187: The Racial Politics of Immigration Law
4. Latino Voters and the 2014 Midterm Elections, Geography, Close Races and Views of Social Issues By Mark Hugo Lopez, Jens Manuel Krogstad, Eileen Patten and Ana Gonzalez-Barrera.
v. Senator Lindsey Graham. NBC Meet the Press. June 8th 2103.
vi. 2004 Presidential Race and Democratic Party.
vii. 2004 Presidential Race and Republican Party.
ix. National Council of La Raza, Annual Conference, Los Angeles. CA July 22nd 2014
x. How Immigration Reform and Demographics Could Change Presidential Math By Nate Silver. April 30. 2013
xi. Congressional Budget Office Report. S774 Bill. 2013
xii. Stepping Up: The Impact of the Newest Immigrant, Asian, and Latino Voters by Rob Paral. Immigration Policy Center Report 2013.
xiii. Gallup Poll. Immigrants and US Born Hispanics. August 2013
xiv. Donald Trump. Washington Times. March 15 2013
xv. Bob Schieffer. CBS This Morning June 13th 2013.

Chapter 10
Conversations on Race, Truth, and Reconciliation in America

> *"The problem [of equality] is so tenacious because, despite its virtues and attributes, America is deeply racist and its democracy is flawed both economically and socially ... justice for Black people cannot be achieved without radical changes in the structure of our society ... exposing evils that are rooted deeply in the whole structure of our society. It reveals systemic rather than superficial flaws and suggests that radical reconstruction of society itself is the real issue to be faced."* [1]
> -Rev. Dr. Martin Luther King, Jr.

The series of seemingly constant, mostly non-violent Black Lives Matter protests throughout America raises uncertainty on the rage, race, and rebellion that continue to plague many African-American communities. These events voice the frustration of the limited upward economic mobility, social despair, disregard for black lives, police brutality, and other social ills that are embedded in many African-American communities. The recent riots address police brutality, but gone from the discussion is the continued economic class warfare that plagues many inner-city communities. The access to upward economic mobility in many African-American communities is the underlying cause of the frustration that has manifested itself in race rebellions and riots. The discussion that America must have is one about how we increase upward economic mobility in a community that has been denied their rightful piece of the American pie. Gone from the dialogue is the impact upward economic mobility has on riots; gone from the dialogue is the continued social oppression that plagues these inner cities; gone from the dialogue is why many African-Americans and their communities are plagued with economic starvation and poverty. These frustrations played an important role in many of the riots in the 1960's, which were often labeled race riots and not class rebellions. The social uprising was part of the economic warfare and disparities that haunted many African-American communities. Yes, race was a factor in the 1960's, but NOT the main underlying source of the frustration found in many African-American communities.

Post racial America is the foremost American dream. With the election of the nation's first African-American President, Americans had great expectations and optimism that they could leave the racial hatred past of the 1950's and 1960's. The dream that America would transcend race, and that racial attitude would undergo a fundamental change, has NOT materialized in the 21st century. Events in Ferguson, Missouri; New York City, New York; Baltimore, Maryland; Orlando, Florida; Charleston, South Carolina; and other parts of the country only reinforce white America's immense racial hatred and distrust in many African-American communities. The dream that we live in a post racial society, where all are guaranteed the benefits of democracy, has been lost in translation. Dialogue about our continued racial reconciliation remains a silent debate, unless another racial event stirs our nation's conscience.

Continued racial events take away the basic foundation of what our democracy stands for: that life, liberty, and the pursuit of happiness are guaranteed to all who live in this promise land. The recent, race-based tragic events have only reminded us that America needs more constructive, open dialogue on its social cancer; RACE.

This social cancer must be addressed in a cautious, sensitive way in which all Americans can have a constructive, meaningful dialogue in order to reach a more proactive resolution. This dialogue must take place throughout all avenues of society, not only when a racial event stirs up racial hatred in our nation. Racial hatred leads to a racially sensitive nation in the short-term, and lost in the dialogue is the long-term solution to America's problem that has been around for the last 300 years.

Recent race based events throughout the country have, once again, left us scrambling for a solution to America's race problem; not only a solution for the earthshaking events of violence, destruction, and disregard for human life, but more so a solution for the frustration in many African-American communities. The riots take us back to the 1960's, when many African-Americans were frustrated with the economic, social, and political disenfranchisement of their American dream. Yes, race was a factor, but not the main underlying source of the frustration in many African-American communities. Baltimore has become the flagship of many poor urban communities. The lack of economic mobility and community policing, and a presence of poverty, drugs, deviant behavior, a failed education system, and continued police brutality continue to plague many inner-city African-American communities. Yes, race was a catalyst, but not the underlying factor of these riots.

The national debate that should take place is not about what threat African-Americans pose to police and society, but more so how we can correct a history of exclusion, oppression, and legal and systematic racism against a community that remains loyal to a country that has treated them as outsiders. Race and race riots take away the best of who we are as Americans, and what we can become as a society. The idea of Americans living in a post-racial society where all races are guaranteed the benefits of the American dream, a society where race and racism no longer exists, has almost disappeared in many urban, minority communities. Thus, there lies the problem among many poor urban cities, these issues, compounded with excessive police distrust and frustration, have led to many of the urban riots we encounter today. The failure to have a constructive dialogue on many of the urban issues that affect African-American communities is the underlying cause of the frustration among many inner-city urban dwellers.

The lack of modern-day policing techniques, community involvement, and communication, but, more so, trust and faith in police fuels much of the debates that should take place today. Historical racism between police forces and African-Americans throughout the country has led to climate of distrust, hate, and disregard for black lives that has fueled much of the frustration that is being depicted today. Baltimore matters because American lives matters; the recent events have only reinforced that race continues to define who we are as Americans, and perpetuates the fact that we are still not living in a post-racial era. These events take away the best of who we are as Americans, and what we can become as a nation.

In the 21st century, many facets of oppression still exist, and are prevalent in many African-American communities; silent, subliminal racism exists in their school systems, employment, poverty, healthcare, prison system, and other sectors of their societies. Class disparities are an important element that defines many black and brown inner cities. In addition, the lack of upward economic mobility opportunities can be easily used to gauge many African-American communities. These economic and class disparities permeate our society in ways we do not even realize, and play an important role in the frustration that plagues many urban communities that African-Americans call home. The access to upward economic mobility is more important today than in any other time in our history, and is the key to bridging many of America's socio-economic and racial gaps. Baltimore and other cities should not be held as the scapegoat for America's socio-economic, political, and race-based problems, but should be held as a leader for the national dialogue that should take place. Baltimore represents much of what it means to be black in America: frustration among America's urban dwellers and poor socio-economic conditions that have led to anger and frustration among its residents. America needs a national discussion about its social ills, not just a discussion in Baltimore. This dialogue must include different races, police officers, community activists, political leaders, members of the clergy, and any other members of urban communities.

The idea of living in a post-racial society where all races are guaranteed the socio-economic benefits of the American dream, and where race and racism no longer exist has almost disappeared in many black and brown communities. African-Americans and other minority groups remain one of the most underrepresented communities in schools, the workforce, and other sectors in American society due to a direct result of economic racism, class discrimination, and their exclusion from the American pie. Baltimore matters because America matters. Black lives matter because American lives matter.

Whatever the arguments are, race, racism, and our economic system have a direct connection, and the underlying issue remains that race plays an important part in all public policy implementation. Economic mobility is one of the main factors that defines many African-American communities, defines who we are as Americans, and has often taken away the best of what we can become as a nation. Yes, race remains an important factor in many of our social ills, but correcting race issues must start with the economic empowerment that is so deeply needed in many of the inner city communities.

The need for America to have a more constructive dialogue has not come to fruition for several factors. First, any discussion of race among white Americans elicits a very cautious and complicated reaction; many whites shy away from any racial dialogue. Second, we must admit we have a problem; a nation that is in denial and is sleepwalking will never wake up. Third, many Americans refuse to acknowledge that racism is a societal problem which can only be resolved by having more open dialogue on race, and discussion on diversity in America. Racial hatred permeates our society in ways we do not even realize, and defines who we are, and what we stand for as nation that leads the free world and preaches democracy.

We, as a nation, must critically evaluate the legacy of the Civil Rights Movement, which primarily fought for the advancement of opportunities of African-Americans: guaranteeing their constitutional rights, eradicating legalized and systematic racism in Jim Crow south, and making America a more racially tolerant society. Have we forgotten this dream? Have we forgotten the message of hope, the foundations of our democracy? Are we, as a nation, suffering from amnesia? It is time to wake up, reflect our wrongdoing and social ills, and make a conscious effort to move forward as a country, and as a people, despite what color we are.

America is still two nations: one white and one black. Only conversations about the truth, the need for reconciliation, and America's acknowledgment of its wrongdoing can lead to a more tolerant society where the American dream can be enjoyed by all.

Reference:
1. http://peoplesworld.org/dr-king-s-last-essay-a-testament-of-hope/

Chapter 11
Conclusion

> *"In the face of hatred, [those in the civil rights movement] prayed for their tormentors. In the face of violence, they stood up and sat in, with the moral force of nonviolence. Willingly, they went to jail to protest unjust laws, their cells swelling with the sound of freedom songs. A lifetime of indignities had taught them that no man can take away the dignity and grace that God grants us. [...] Because they marched, America became more free and more fair -- not just for African-Americans, but for women and Latinos, Asians and Native Americans; for Catholics, Jews, and Muslims; for gays, for Americans with a disability. America changed for you and for me."* [1]
> -President Barack Obama. August 28, 2013

At no other time in our country's great history has an idea of a post-racial society caught the eye of many Americans; yet this vision has neither materialized nor even blossomed. Many argue the emergence of an African-American candidate has fueled the debate regarding where race and politics fit in America. The increased expectations that America would transcend beyond race and that racial attitudes would undergo a fundamental change, despite this expectation, it has not. Race continues to play an important role in America's society, recent race based events throughout the country have left us gasping for a solution for America's social cancer. These events have only reinforced that race continues to define who we are as Americans and perpetuate the fact that we are not living in a post racial society in the age of Obama.

As we all looked at the swearing of the nation's first African-American President into office, the idea was that America was willing to put its ugly past behind and move towards a post racial society becoming a more racially tolerant nation. The idea that America in the post racial Obama's presidency would become a melting pot that we constantly reminded off and often embrace remains a distant dream. Despite this idea of a post racial society, race and racism continue to be alive and well in America and the fact that we are not living in a post racial era continues to be a major disappointment in our country.

As America slowly but surely confronts the issue of race, it becomes quite clear that race still matters in America. As we entered the 21st-century silent and not overt segregation exists in our school systems, employment, poverty, healthcare, prison system, immigrant communities, and other sectors of societies. It also permeates our society in ways we don't even realize and is defined in every American public policy. Integration of schools, hotels, workforce, parks, public places and other avenues of society has left a blind eye to many of hidden racial disparities that are prevalent in American society. Race and racism continues to perpetuate in our society despite having our first African-American president and recent events throughout the country only reinforce the significance of race in America.

The idea of Americans living in a post racial society where all races are guaranteed the benefits of the American Dream and a society where race and racism no longer exists have almost disappeared in many minority communities. African-Americans and other minority groups remain one of the most underrepresented communities in schools, workforce, and other sectors in the American society. The issue remains why are we not living in a post racial society? Why is race so important in America? Can we achieve a post racial society in America?

There is no definite answer to solving our post racial problem but here lies some of our obstacles towards achieving the dream of a post racial America. First, any discussion of race among Americans illicit a very cautious and complicated reaction; many of whom often shy away from any constructive dialogue. Second, admitting that we have a problem; a nation that is in denial and is sleepwalking will never wake up, and thirdly, many Americans refuse to acknowledge that racism is a societal problem which can be only resolved by having more open dialogue on race and discussion on diversity in America. Only conversations about the truth, the need for reconciliation, and America's acknowledgment of its past wrongdoing can lead to a more racially tolerant society in the 21st century.

Thus, here lies the problem of why post racial America has been lost in translation and why race still matters. Race relations have taken away the best of who we are as Americans and what we can become as a society. Failure to talk about America's social cancer, failure to admit that race is a societal problem is what fuels the continuing significance of race in post Obama presidency. The election of our first African-American President has demonstrated our great strides towards a racial harmonious society, where we respect all the contributions to our great country. There needs to be a conversations about the America's past relationship with African-Americans, the need for reconciliation, forgiveness, and America's acknowledgment of its wrongdoing. This will only lead to a more racially tolerant country where the American dream can be enjoyed by all and then the idea of a post racial society can be achieved.

Recent protests by several African-American athletes, with regard to respecting the American national anthem and flag, have once again left us as a nation searching for an American identity. Who are we, and where do the roles of racial politics and African-American patriotism fit in with the nation? The idea of a post-racial America continues to be lost in translation; race continues to be a significant factor as we delve into the deep waters of American patriotism and African-Americans. This debate has not only generated dialogue about the continued role that race plays in our society, but has also posed the question of whether African-Americans are truly committed to the *"Land of the free and the home of the brave."* The African-American commitment to protecting democracy and freedom, the basic watch-words of the anthem and symbol of the flag, is lost in history books. In fact, most Americans are unaware that the first casualty in the Revolutionary War of 1776 was an African-American named Crispus Attucks, in what is often termed the Boston Massacre. African-Americans have put their lives on the line to protect their freedom, liberty, and democracy in the Revolutionary War, Civil War, World War I, World War II, Vietnam, and the present-day wars in Iraq and Afghanistan; African-Americans have played a vital role in every military conflict: every war, every battle, and on every battlefield. It must be noted that African-Americans have always met the challenge of serving America with great pride, commitment, and admiration, yet they continue to face racial backlash in a country that has refused to come to terms with their racial presence.

The debate that should be taking place is not whether African-Americans are patriotic to America, but whether America has been fair to African-Americans; has America lived up to their ideals, acknowledged their culture, and embraced the African-American experience? After all, what would America be like without African-Americans? Francis Scott Key, like many other prominent Americans of the time, profited from the institution of slavery. Key even owned slaves, yet he penned *"Land of the Free, Home of the Brave,"* which became our national anthem in 1931. Like Scott Key, Thomas Jefferson, the architect of our famed Declaration of Independence that preached *"That all men are created equal,"* owned some three-hundred slaves, and denied enslaved African-Americans life, liberty, and the pursuit of happiness. The point is, that America has always contradicted its founding values, in regards to African-Americans. America and African-Americans have always had a love-hate relationship, which stems from the contradiction of our basic watch-words and foundations manifested in our national anthem and flag. The issue should NOT be whether African-Americans are loyal to America, that question was answered when the first slave ship arrived in Jamestown, VA in 1619, but whether America has been loyal to, and fair towards African Americans?

Racism and race relations continue to define many of our public policies and play an important role in every sector of society whether we admit it or not. We should be very proud of our accomplishments, our strides towards a post racial society, our Civil Rights gains; but it is also important that we do not become complacent with this progress. Post-racial America and achieving meaningful Civil Rights is a far-fetched dream that continues to elude us and takes away the best of what we stand for as Americans.

Reference:
1. http://peoplesworld.org/dr-king-s-last-essay-a-testament-of-hope/

About the Author

Stephen Balkaran, is currently an Instructor of African-American Studies at Central Connecticut State University (2006-Pres), where he initiated, developed and coordinate a Civil Rights Project. He also serves as an Instructor of Political Science at Quinnipiac University (2011-Pres), The University of Connecticut-TRI CAMPUS (2005-06), Post University (2003-04), and Capital Community College (1999-03). He has also served as Research Fellow for, The Human Rights Research Fund at Yale University, working under Black Panther and Yale Professor of African-American Studies, Mrs. Kathleen Cleaver.

He has authored 4 books: Broken Promises, Broken Dreams: Disparities and Disappointments: Civil Rights in the 21st Century, Before We Were Called Hispanics: Conversations on the Race, Politics, & Immigration Reform, The Continuing Significance of Race: An American Dilemma, and

Re-Tracing the Civil Rights Movement. His 5th and forthcoming book is titled; Trouble in Paradise: African- Americans and the Politics of Race in Key West, FL. Also, he has authored over 60 articles in Academic Journals, Magazines, and OP-EDs on Race Relations, Diversity & Inclusion, American Foreign Policy, and Public Policy. He has also given over 75 speeches on his research, publications, and books throughout the United States.

Before launching his academic career, Mr. Balkaran, worked for the African National Congress *(Nelson Mandela's ruling party in South Africa)* in partnership with the University of Connecticut. He was also a Research Associate for the United Nations in New York, and was a former Legislative Aide to the CT Secretary of the State.

Mr. Balkaran's educational background spans from the Presentation College in Trinidad, The University of Connecticut, and Quinnipiac University School of Law. Mr. Balkaran, currently resides in Hartford, CT. USA and is a native of Trinidad & Tobago.